Axton Nexus

Computer Graphics Development With DirectX

A Complete Beginner's Guide to Building High-Performance, Real-Time 3D Graphics Applications for Games, Simulations, and Visualizations

Table Of Contents

Disclaimer

While every effort has been made to ensure the accuracy and completeness of the information within this book, the author and publisher make no warranty, express or implied, with respect to the content, and specifically disclaim any implied warranties of merchantability or fitness for a particular purpose. The[1] author and publisher shall not be liable for any direct, indirect, incidental, special, consequential, or exemplary damages arising out of the use[2] of this book, even if advised of the possibility of such damages.

The code examples provided in this book are intended for illustrative purposes and may require modifications to function correctly in specific environments or applications. It is the reader's responsibility to adapt and test the code as needed.

DirectX is a registered trademark of Microsoft Corporation. All other trademarks and registered trademarks are the property of their respective owners.[3]

This book is intended for educational purposes and does not constitute professional advice. The reader should consult qualified professionals for specific guidance on their projects or applications.

The information contained in this book is subject to change without notice. The author and publisher are not responsible for any errors or omissions that may occur.

By reading and using this book, you agree to the terms of this disclaimer.

In Plain English:

We've done our best to make this book awesome and accurate, but stuff happens! We can't guarantee that every single thing will work perfectly for everyone, and we're not responsible if something goes wrong. Use your best judgment, test your code, and have fun learning DirectX!

Introduction

Imagine stepping into a world where the only limit to visual fidelity is your imagination. Where light dances realistically off surfaces, shadows deepen with nuance, and characters move with lifelike fluidity. This is the world DirectX unlocks, and it's a world ripe with opportunity for game developers, IT professionals, graphics programmers, and software engineers alike.

But DirectX can seem daunting, a labyrinth of APIs and cryptic acronyms. Fear not! This book is your guide, meticulously crafted to illuminate the path to mastering DirectX and harnessing its immense power.

Why is this journey crucial now? Because the landscape of interactive experiences is transforming at an unprecedented pace. Ray tracing, once a distant dream, is now a reality in games like *Cyberpunk 2077* and *Control*, casting realistic reflections and shadows that blur the lines between the virtual and the real. Virtual and augmented reality are no longer niche technologies, with devices like the Meta Quest and Apple Vision Pro pushing the boundaries of immersive experiences. And AI is seeping into every facet of graphics, from generating stunning visuals to powering intelligent game characters.

To stay ahead of the curve, to craft the next generation of groundbreaking games and applications, you need DirectX in your arsenal. This book equips you with the knowledge and skills to not just understand DirectX, but to wield it with confidence and creativity.

Whether you're a seasoned game developer seeking to elevate your visuals, an IT professional exploring new avenues, or a curious programmer eager to delve into the world of graphics, this book is your gateway.

Prepare to embark on a journey that will transform your perspective on what's possible. Get ready to master DirectX, and unleash the power to create breathtaking digital worlds.

Part I: Foundations

Chapter 1: Introduction to Computer Graphics

What is Computer Graphics?

Computer graphics is the art and science of creating, manipulating, and displaying visual content using computers. It's a field that blends creativity and technical expertise, enabling us to generate images, animations, and interactive visual experiences that entertain, inform, and inspire.

At its core, computer graphics involves using mathematical algorithms and data structures to represent and manipulate visual information. This information can take many forms, from simple geometric shapes to complex 3D models, and from static images to dynamic animations.

The Essence of Computer Graphics

Imagine a painter using brushes and pigments to create a masterpiece on canvas. In computer graphics, the "canvas" is the computer screen, the "brushes" are the algorithms and software tools, and the "pigments" are the digital data that defines colors, shapes, and textures.

Instead of physically applying paint, computer graphics relies on calculations and instructions to generate images. These instructions tell the computer how to arrange pixels on the screen, creating the illusion of lines, shapes, and colors.

Key Concepts

To understand computer graphics, it's essential to grasp a few fundamental concepts:

- **Pixels:** The tiny dots that make up a digital image. Each pixel has a specific color and position on the screen.
- **Resolution:** The number of pixels in an image, determining its clarity and detail. Higher resolution means more pixels and a sharper image.
- **Color Models:** Systems for representing colors digitally, such as RGB (Red, Green, Blue) and CMYK (Cyan, Magenta, Yellow, Key/Black).
- **Geometry:** The mathematical representation of shapes, including points, lines, curves, and polygons.
- **Rendering:** The process of converting a mathematical description of a scene into a 2D image.

Types of Computer Graphics

Computer graphics encompasses a wide range of techniques and applications, including:

- **2D Graphics:** Creating and manipulating images in two dimensions, such as illustrations, logos, and user interfaces.
- **3D Graphics:** Generating and rendering three-dimensional objects and scenes, used in games, movies, and simulations.
- **Animation:** Creating the illusion of movement by displaying a sequence of images.
- **Image Processing:** Analyzing and modifying existing images, such as enhancing photos or applying filters.
- **Visualization:** Representing data graphically to aid understanding and analysis.

Applications of Computer Graphics

Computer graphics has become an indispensable tool in various fields, including:

- **Entertainment:** Video games, animated movies, special effects in films.
- **Design:** Architectural visualization, product design, graphic design.
- **Education:** Interactive simulations, educational software, visualizations.

- **Science and Engineering:** Scientific visualization, medical imaging, simulations.
- **Medicine:** Medical imaging, surgical planning, patient education.

The Role of DirectX

DirectX is a powerful set of APIs (Application Programming Interfaces) developed by Microsoft specifically for multimedia and gaming applications on Windows platforms. It provides a comprehensive toolkit for graphics programmers to access hardware resources and create high-performance graphics applications.

In this book, we'll focus on using DirectX to develop real-time 3D graphics applications, primarily for games, simulations, and visualizations.

Moving Forward

In the next section, we'll delve into the mathematical foundations of computer graphics, exploring the essential concepts that underpin the creation and manipulation of visual content.

Applications of Computer Graphics (Games, Simulations, Visualization, etc.)

Computer graphics has permeated nearly every aspect of our digital lives, and its applications are incredibly diverse and constantly expanding. Here's a glimpse into some of the key areas where computer graphics plays a crucial role:

1. Entertainment

This is perhaps the most widely recognized application of computer graphics. It has revolutionized the entertainment industry, bringing us immersive and captivating experiences:

- **Video Games:** From the pixelated sprites of early arcade games to the photorealistic worlds of modern AAA titles, computer graphics is the driving force behind interactive entertainment. It enables the creation of lifelike characters, stunning environments, and dynamic visual effects that engage players and transport them to virtual realms.
- **Animated Movies:** Computer animation has transformed the way stories are told on screen. Pixar, DreamWorks, and other studios leverage powerful graphics software to create beloved

characters and breathtaking worlds, pushing the boundaries of visual storytelling.

- **Special Effects in Films:** Computer-generated imagery (CGI) has become an integral part of filmmaking. From subtle enhancements to spectacular action sequences, CGI seamlessly blends with live-action footage to create realistic and fantastical effects that enhance the cinematic experience.

2. Design and Engineering

Computer graphics is an indispensable tool for designers and engineers across various disciplines:

- **Computer-Aided Design (CAD):** Architects, engineers, and product designers use CAD software to create precise 2D and 3D models of buildings, vehicles, machinery, and other objects. This allows for accurate visualization, analysis, and modification of designs before they are physically built.
- **Architectural Visualization:** Realistic renderings and walkthroughs of architectural designs help clients and stakeholders visualize spaces and understand the aesthetics and functionality of proposed buildings.
- **Product Design:** From consumer electronics to automobiles, computer graphics aids in

visualizing and refining product designs, ensuring both form and function are optimized.

3. Education and Training

Computer graphics enhances learning and skill development through interactive and engaging experiences:

- **Interactive Simulations:** Simulations of real-world scenarios, such as flight simulators or medical training programs, allow users to practice skills and learn in a safe and controlled environment.
- **Educational Software:** Interactive visualizations and animations help students grasp complex concepts and engage with learning materials in a more dynamic way.
- **Virtual Field Trips:** Immersive virtual reality experiences can transport students to distant locations or historical periods, providing unique educational opportunities.

4. Science and Medicine

Computer graphics plays a vital role in scientific research, medical diagnosis, and treatment:

- **Scientific Visualization:** Complex scientific data, such as weather patterns, molecular structures, or astronomical phenomena, can be visualized using computer graphics to aid in analysis and understanding.

- **Medical Imaging:** Techniques like MRI and CT scans produce 3D images of the human body, allowing doctors to diagnose injuries and diseases with greater accuracy.
- **Surgical Planning:** Surgeons can use 3D models generated from medical images to plan complex procedures and visualize potential challenges before entering the operating room.

5. Visualization and Data Analysis

Computer graphics helps us make sense of large datasets and complex information:

- **Data Visualization:** Charts, graphs, and interactive visualizations transform raw data into meaningful insights, revealing patterns, trends, and relationships.
- **Information Graphics:** Visually compelling infographics communicate complex information in a clear and concise manner.
- **Financial Modeling:** Computer graphics is used to visualize financial data, market trends, and risk assessments.

Beyond the Basics

The applications of computer graphics continue to evolve with advancements in technology. Emerging fields like virtual reality (VR) and augmented reality (AR) are pushing the boundaries of interactive experiences, while artificial intelligence (AI) is being integrated with computer graphics to create intelligent and adaptive visual systems.

As you delve deeper into the world of computer graphics, you'll discover countless opportunities to apply your skills and creativity to solve problems, create innovative solutions, and contribute to a wide range of industries.

Evolution of Computer Graphics

The journey of computer graphics is a fascinating tale of innovation, driven by the desire to visualize and interact with data in increasingly sophisticated ways. From its humble beginnings to the stunning realism of today, here's a glimpse into the key milestones that have shaped this field:

Early Days (1950s - 1960s):

- **The First Steps:** The earliest forms of computer graphics were rudimentary line drawings and basic shapes displayed on cathode ray tube (CRT) monitors. These were primarily used for scientific and military purposes, such as plotting data and simulating trajectories.

- **Pioneering Innovations:** Ivan Sutherland's Sketchpad (1963) is considered a landmark achievement. It was the first interactive graphics program, allowing users to draw and manipulate objects on a computer screen using a light pen. This laid the foundation for computer-aided design (CAD) and human-computer interaction.

Emergence of 3D and Realism (1970s - 1980s):

- **The Dawn of 3D:** Researchers began exploring techniques to represent and render three-dimensional objects. Early 3D models were often wireframe representations, lacking surface details and realistic lighting.
- **Shading and Rendering:** New algorithms like Gouraud shading and Phong shading were developed to simulate the interaction of light with surfaces, adding a sense of depth and realism to 3D graphics.
- **Early Animation:** Computer animation took its first steps with films like "Tron" (1982), showcasing the potential of CGI in storytelling.

The Rise of Real-time Graphics (1990s):

- **The GPU Revolution:** The introduction of dedicated graphics processing units (GPUs) marked a turning point. GPUs accelerated graphics rendering, enabling real-time 3D graphics in video games and interactive applications.

- **Gaming Takes Center Stage:** Games like "Doom" and "Quake" popularized 3D graphics, driving innovation in rendering techniques and pushing the boundaries of visual fidelity.
- **Standardization and APIs:** Graphics APIs like OpenGL and DirectX emerged, providing standardized ways for software to communicate with graphics hardware, fostering cross-platform development.

Modern Era (2000s - Present):

- **Photorealism and Beyond:** Advancements in rendering algorithms, lighting models, and texture mapping have enabled the creation of incredibly realistic images and animations, blurring the lines between virtual and real.
- **Rise of New Technologies:** Virtual reality (VR), augmented reality (AR), and mixed reality (MR) are creating immersive and interactive experiences, transforming how we interact with digital content.
- **AI and Graphics:** Artificial intelligence is being integrated with computer graphics to automate tasks, generate content, and enhance realism.

The Future of Computer Graphics:

The evolution of computer graphics continues at a rapid pace. We can expect to see even more realistic and immersive experiences, driven by:

- **Real-time Ray Tracing:** Simulating the physical behavior of light for stunningly accurate reflections and shadows.
- **Cloud-based Graphics:** Leveraging the power of cloud computing to render complex scenes and stream high-fidelity graphics to various devices.
- **AI-powered Creation:** Using AI to generate realistic 3D models, textures, and animations, simplifying content creation workflows.

As you embark on your journey into the world of computer graphics, remember that you're stepping into a field with a rich history and a bright future. By understanding its evolution, you'll gain a deeper appreciation for the techniques and technologies that shape the visual experiences we enjoy today and those that will redefine our digital world tomorrow.

Why DirectX?

While there are other graphics APIs available (like OpenGL and Vulkan), DirectX holds a special place in the world of Windows development, especially for games. Here's why it's a compelling choice for your graphics programming journey:

1. Windows-Centric Optimization:

- **Deep Integration:** DirectX is developed by Microsoft specifically for Windows and Xbox. This tight integration with the operating system and hardware often leads to superior performance and stability on Windows platforms.
- **Access to Latest Features:** DirectX often provides early access to the latest graphics features and hardware advancements from companies like NVIDIA and AMD. This gives developers a cutting edge, especially when working with new technologies like ray tracing.

2. Comprehensive Feature Set:

- **More Than Just Graphics:** DirectX is a collection of APIs that go beyond 3D rendering. It includes components for audio processing (DirectSound), input handling (DirectInput), networking (DirectPlay), and more. This provides a unified framework for multimedia development.
- **Rich Functionality:** DirectX offers a wide range of built-in features and utilities that simplify common graphics programming tasks. This can

save you time and effort compared to implementing everything from scratch with other APIs.

3. Ease of Use (Relatively Speaking):

- **Simplified Abstraction:** DirectX provides a higher level of abstraction compared to some other APIs. This can make it easier to get started and achieve results quickly, especially for beginners.
- **Excellent Documentation and Support:** Microsoft provides comprehensive documentation, tutorials, and sample code for DirectX. You'll find a wealth of resources to help you learn and troubleshoot issues.
- **Large Community:** DirectX has a large and active community of developers. This means you can find answers to your questions, share knowledge, and get support from fellow programmers.

4. Industry Standard for Games:

- **Dominant in Game Development:** DirectX is the dominant graphics API in the Windows gaming ecosystem. Most AAA game studios rely on DirectX, and many game engines (like Unreal Engine and Unity) have robust DirectX support.

- **Career Relevance:** Learning DirectX enhances your career prospects in the game development industry. It's a valuable skill sought after by many game studios.

5. Continuous Improvement:

- **Active Development:** Microsoft continues to invest in and improve DirectX. New versions with enhanced features and performance optimizations are regularly released.
- **Future-Proofing:** By learning DirectX, you're investing in a technology with a strong future. Microsoft's commitment to DirectX ensures its relevance in the evolving landscape of graphics programming.

Choosing the Right Tool:

While DirectX is a powerful and versatile API, it's worth noting that other APIs like OpenGL and Vulkan have their own strengths, particularly in cross-platform development. The choice of API often depends on the specific needs of your project and your target platforms.

For this book, we'll focus on DirectX because it's an excellent choice for beginners who want to learn graphics programming on Windows and explore the exciting world of game development.

Setting Up Your Development Environment (Visual Studio, Windows SDK)

Before you dive into the exciting world of DirectX programming, it's essential to set up a proper development environment on your Windows machine. This involves installing the necessary software and tools, configuring settings, and ensuring everything works seamlessly. Here's a step-by-step guide to get you started:

1. Install Visual Studio:

- **The IDE of Choice:** Visual Studio is the recommended Integrated Development Environment (IDE) for DirectX development. It provides a comprehensive set of tools for coding, debugging, and building applications.
- **Download and Installation:** Download the latest version of Visual Studio from the official Microsoft website (visualstudio.microsoft.com). During installation, make sure to select the following workloads:
  - **"Desktop development with C++"** This includes the core C++ tools and libraries necessary for DirectX programming.
  - **"Universal Windows Platform development"** This allows you to create

applications that can run on a variety of Windows devices.

2. Install the Windows SDK:

- **Essential Components:** The Windows SDK (Software Development Kit) provides header files, libraries, and tools for developing Windows applications, including those that use DirectX.
- **Included with Visual Studio:** The Windows SDK is typically included when you install Visual Studio. However, it's good practice to check for updates to ensure you have the latest version. You can do this through the Visual Studio Installer.

3. Configure Visual Studio for DirectX:

- **Create a New Project:** Start by creating a new project in Visual Studio. Choose "Visual C++" -> "Windows Desktop" -> "Windows Desktop Application" as your project template.
- **Include DirectX Headers:** To use DirectX in your project, you need to include the necessary header files. In your source code files, add the following line at the top:

```
C++

#include <d3d12.h>
```

- **Link DirectX Libraries:** You also need to link your project with the DirectX libraries. Go to Project -> Properties -> Linker -> Input -> Additional Dependencies and add the following:

d3d12.lib; dxgi.lib; d3dcompiler.lib

4. Verify Your Setup:

- **Compile a Simple Program:** To ensure everything is set up correctly, create a simple DirectX program (like the "Hello, DirectX!" example that draws a triangle) and try to compile and run it.
- **Troubleshooting:** If you encounter errors, double-check that you've installed the correct workloads and components, included the necessary headers, and linked the required libraries.

Additional Tips:

- **Keep Your Software Updated:** Regularly check for updates to Visual Studio and the Windows SDK to ensure you have the latest features and bug fixes.
- **Explore DirectX Samples:** Microsoft provides a variety of DirectX sample projects that you can download and study. These can be a valuable resource for learning different DirectX techniques.
- **Join the DirectX Community:** Engage with the DirectX community through forums, online communities, and social media. You can find answers to your questions, share knowledge, and get support from fellow developers.

With your development environment set up, you're now ready to embark on your DirectX programming journey! In the next chapter, we'll delve into the mathematical foundations of computer graphics, which will be crucial for understanding how to create and manipulate visual content.

Chapter 2: Mathematics for Graphics

Coordinate Systems and Transformations

Mathematics forms the backbone of computer graphics, providing the language and tools to describe and manipulate visual elements in a digital world.[1] In this chapter, we'll explore the fundamental concepts of coordinate systems and transformations, which are essential for understanding how objects are positioned, oriented, and moved within a graphical environment.

Coordinate Systems: Defining the Where

A coordinate system provides a framework for representing the location of points and objects in space.[2] In computer graphics, we primarily deal with two types of coordinate systems:

1. Cartesian Coordinate System:

- **The Familiar Grid:** This system uses perpendicular axes (usually labeled X, Y, and Z in 3D) to define a grid.[3] Each point in space is uniquely identified by its coordinates along these axes.[4]
- **2D vs. 3D:** In 2D graphics, we use the X and Y axes to represent points on a flat plane.[5] In 3D

graphics, we add the Z-axis to represent depth
and create a three-dimensional space.[6]

2. Homogeneous Coordinates:

- **Adding Dimensionality:** This system extends
  the Cartesian system by adding an extra
  dimension (usually denoted as W).[7] This allows
  us to represent points at infinity and perform
  perspective transformations efficiently.
- **Perspective and Projections:** Homogeneous
  coordinates are crucial for projecting 3D scenes
  onto a 2D screen, creating the illusion of depth
  and perspective.[8]

Transformations: Manipulating Objects in Space

Transformations are mathematical operations that alter
the position, orientation, or size of objects within a
coordinate system.[9] They are fundamental to animation,
scene composition, and creating dynamic visual
experiences.[10]

1. Basic Transformations:

- **Translation:** Moving an object from one location
  to another without changing its orientation or
  size.[11]
- **Rotation:** Rotating an object around a specific
  axis (X, Y, or Z) by a certain angle.[12]

- **Scaling:** Enlarging or shrinking an object uniformly or along specific axes.

2. Combining Transformations:

- **Matrix Representation:** Transformations are typically represented using matrices.[13] This allows us to combine multiple transformations into a single matrix, making calculations efficient.[14]
- **Order Matters:** The order in which transformations are applied can significantly affect the final result.[15] Experimentation and understanding the order of operations are crucial.

3. Transformation Matrices:

- **Mathematical Representation:** Each basic transformation (translation, rotation, scaling) has a corresponding matrix representation.[16] These matrices are used to perform the transformations on points or objects.[17]
- **4x4 Matrices for 3D:** In 3D graphics, we use 4x4 matrices to represent transformations in homogeneous coordinates.[18] This allows us to handle perspective projections and combine various transformations effectively.

4. World, View, and Projection Transformations:

- **World Transformation:** Positions objects within the world coordinate system.
- **View Transformation:** Defines the position and orientation of the camera in the world.[19]
- **Projection Transformation:** Projects the 3D scene onto the 2D screen, creating the illusion of perspective.

Applying Transformations in DirectX:

DirectX provides functions and methods for applying transformations to objects within your graphics applications.[20] You'll learn how to use matrices to translate, rotate, and scale objects, as well as how to set up camera views and project 3D scenes onto the screen.

Moving Forward:

Understanding coordinate systems and transformations is crucial for effectively manipulating objects and creating dynamic scenes in your DirectX applications. In the next chapter, we'll dive into the heart of DirectX and explore the graphics pipeline, which is the series of steps involved in rendering images on the screen.

Vectors and Matrices

Vectors and matrices are fundamental mathematical objects that play a central role in computer graphics. They provide a powerful way to represent and manipulate points, directions, and transformations in space.

Vectors: Representing Direction and Magnitude

A vector is a mathematical entity that has both magnitude (length) and direction. Think of it as an arrow pointing in space. In computer graphics, vectors are used to represent various quantities, including:

- **Positions:** The location of a point in space relative to an origin.
- **Directions:** The orientation of an object or the direction of movement.
- **Displacements:** The change in position from one point to another.
- **Normals:** Vectors perpendicular to a surface, used for lighting calculations.

Vector Operations:

Vectors can be added, subtracted, scaled, and combined in various ways:

- **Addition:** Combining two vectors to get a resultant vector.
- **Subtraction:** Finding the difference between two vectors.

- **Scalar Multiplication:** Scaling the length of a vector by multiplying it with a scalar (a single number).
- **Dot Product:** Calculating the angle between two vectors or projecting one vector onto another.
- **Cross Product:** Finding a vector perpendicular to two given vectors, useful for determining surface normals.

Matrices: Organizing Numbers and Transformations

A matrix is a rectangular array of numbers arranged in rows and columns. In computer graphics, matrices are primarily used for:

- **Representing Transformations:** Matrices provide a concise way to represent transformations like translation, rotation, and scaling.
- **Transforming Vectors:** Multiplying a vector by a transformation matrix applies that transformation to the vector.
- **Combining Transformations:** Multiplying transformation matrices together combines those transformations into a single operation.

Matrix Operations:

Matrices can be added, subtracted, multiplied, and manipulated in various ways:

- **Addition:** Adding corresponding elements of two matrices.
- **Subtraction:** Subtracting corresponding elements of two matrices.
- **Scalar Multiplication:** Multiplying each element of a matrix by a scalar.
- **Matrix Multiplication:** A more complex operation that combines rows and columns of two matrices. This is crucial for combining transformations.
- **Transpose:** Switching rows and columns of a matrix.
- **Inverse:** Finding a matrix that, when multiplied with the original matrix, results in the identity matrix (a matrix with 1s on the diagonal and 0s elsewhere).

Why Vectors and Matrices are Essential in Graphics:

- **Efficiency:** Matrices allow for efficient representation and combination of transformations.
- **Conciseness:** Complex transformations can be represented by a single matrix.
- **Hardware Optimization:** GPUs are optimized for matrix operations, enabling fast and efficient graphics rendering.

Using Vectors and Matrices in DirectX:

DirectX provides data types and functions for working with vectors and matrices. You'll use them extensively to:

- **Define object positions and orientations.**
- **Apply transformations to objects.**
- **Set up camera views and projections.**
- **Perform lighting calculations.**

Moving Forward:

Mastering vectors and matrices is crucial for understanding and implementing transformations in your DirectX applications. In the next section, we'll explore linear algebra essentials, which provide the foundation for working with vectors and matrices in a graphical context.

Linear Algebra Essentials

Linear algebra provides the mathematical foundation for many concepts in computer graphics, particularly when dealing with vectors, matrices, and transformations. Here, we'll cover the essential linear algebra concepts you'll need for your DirectX journey.

1. Vectors:

- **Vector Space:** A collection of vectors that can be added together and multiplied by scalars (real numbers), obeying certain rules (like commutativity and associativity).

- **Linear Combination:** A sum of scalar multiples of vectors. For example, $v = 2a + 3b$ is a linear combination of vectors a and b.
- **Linear Independence:** A set of vectors is linearly independent if none of them can be expressed as a linear combination of the others.[1]
- **Basis:** A set of linearly independent vectors that can span the entire vector space. Any vector in the space can be expressed as a unique linear combination of the basis vectors.

2. Matrices:

- **Matrix Operations:** Review the matrix operations from the previous section (addition, subtraction, scalar multiplication, matrix multiplication). Understand how matrix multiplication works and its non-commutative nature (A * B is generally not equal to B * A).
- **Identity Matrix:** A square matrix with 1s on the diagonal and 0s elsewhere. Multiplying any matrix by the identity matrix leaves it unchanged.
- **Inverse Matrix:** A matrix that, when multiplied with the original matrix, results in the identity matrix. Used to reverse transformations.

3. Systems of Linear Equations:

- **Solving Equations:** Linear algebra provides techniques for solving systems of linear equations. This is useful in graphics for tasks like finding intersections of lines and planes.
- **Matrix Representation:** Systems of linear equations can be represented compactly using matrices.

4. Determinants:

- **Scaling Factor:** The determinant of a matrix is a scalar value that represents the scaling factor of the transformation represented by the matrix.[2]
- **Invertibility:** A matrix is invertible (has an inverse) if and only if its determinant is non-zero.

5. Eigenvectors and Eigenvalues:

- **Special Vectors:** An eigenvector of a matrix is a non-zero vector that, when multiplied by the matrix, only changes by a scalar factor (the eigenvalue).
- **Applications:** Eigenvectors and eigenvalues have applications in graphics for tasks like principal component analysis and deformation.

Why Linear Algebra Matters in Graphics:

- **Transformations:** Transformations like translation, rotation, and scaling are represented and applied using matrices.

- **Coordinate Systems:** Understanding vector spaces and basis vectors is crucial for working with different coordinate systems.
- **Geometric Calculations:** Linear algebra provides tools for performing geometric calculations like finding intersections, distances, and projections.
- **3D Graphics:** Many 3D graphics concepts rely heavily on linear algebra, including projections, lighting, and animation.

Moving Forward:

A solid grasp of linear algebra essentials will significantly enhance your ability to understand and implement graphics techniques in DirectX. In the next chapter, we'll introduce you to the core concepts of DirectX and the graphics pipeline, setting the stage for your journey into the world of 3D graphics programming.

3D Transformations (Translation, Rotation, Scaling)

3D transformations are the building blocks for manipulating objects within a three-dimensional space. They allow you to position, orient, and resize objects to create dynamic and engaging scenes. Let's explore the three fundamental 3D transformations: translation, rotation, and scaling.

1. Translation

Translation involves moving an object from one point in space to another without changing its orientation or size. Think of it as sliding an object along a straight path.

- **Mathematical Representation:** In 3D, translation is represented by adding a translation vector (tx, ty, tz) to the original coordinates (x, y, z) of each point in the object:

$x' = x + tx$

$y' = y + ty$

$z' = z + tz$

- **Matrix Representation:** Translation can be efficiently represented using a 4x4 translation matrix in homogeneous coordinates:

[1 0 0 tx]

[0 1 0 ty]

$$[0\ 0\ 1\ \ tz\ ]$$

$$[0\ 0\ 0\ 1\ ]$$

To apply the translation, you multiply this matrix with the homogeneous coordinates of the point (x, y, z, 1).

2. Rotation

Rotation involves turning an object around a specific axis (X, Y, or Z) by a certain angle.

- **Axis of Rotation:** The axis of rotation determines the direction in which the object rotates.
- **Angle of Rotation:** The angle of rotation specifies how much the object is turned.
- **Matrix Representation:** Rotation is represented by different 4x4 rotation matrices depending on the axis of rotation:
  - **Rotation around X-axis:**

$$[\ 1\ 0\ \ \ \ 0\ \ \ \ \ 0\ ]$$

$$[\ 0\ \cos(\theta)\ -\sin(\theta)\ \ 0\ ]$$

$$[\ 0\ \sin(\theta)\ \ \cos(\theta)\ \ 0\ ]$$

[0 0   0   1]

- **Rotation around Y-axis:**

[cos(θ) 0 sin(θ) 0]

[0   1 0   0]

[-sin(θ) 0 cos(θ) 0]

[0   0 0   1]

- **Rotation around Z-axis:**

[cos(θ) -sin(θ) 0 0]

[sin(θ) cos(θ) 0 0]

[0   0   1 0]

[0   0   0 1]

- To apply the rotation, you multiply the appropriate rotation matrix with the homogeneous coordinates of the point.

3. Scaling

Scaling involves resizing an object, either uniformly or along specific axes.

- **Scaling Factors:** Scaling factors (sx, sy, sz) determine how much the object is scaled along each axis.
- **Matrix Representation:** Scaling is represented by a 4x4 scaling matrix:

[sx 0 0 0]

[0 sy 0 0]

[0 0 sz 0]

[0 0 0 1]

To apply the scaling, you multiply this matrix with the homogeneous coordinates of the point.

Combining Transformations

You can combine multiple transformations by multiplying their corresponding matrices. Remember that the order of multiplication matters, as matrix multiplication is not commutative.

Applying Transformations in DirectX

DirectX provides functions and methods for creating and applying transformation matrices to objects in your scenes. You'll typically use these matrices to:

- **Position objects in the world.**
- **Control the camera's view.**
- **Project the 3D scene onto the 2D screen.**

Moving Forward:

Understanding and mastering 3D transformations is fundamental to creating dynamic and interactive graphics applications. In the next chapter, we'll delve into the heart of DirectX and explore the graphics pipeline, which is the series of steps involved in rendering images on the screen.

Chapter 3: Introduction to DirectX

DirectX Components (Direct3D, Direct2D, etc.)

DirectX isn't just about 3D graphics; it's a comprehensive suite of APIs designed to empower developers in creating multimedia-rich applications, especially games. It provides a unified framework for accessing hardware resources and handling various aspects of multimedia, including graphics, audio, input, and networking. Let's explore some of the key components that make DirectX such a versatile tool:

1. Direct3D: The Heart of 3D Graphics

Direct3D (D3D) is the core component of DirectX responsible for hardware-accelerated 3D graphics rendering. It provides a low-level interface for interacting with graphics processing units (GPUs) and enables developers to create stunning visual experiences in games, simulations, and visualizations.

- **Key Features:**
  - **Hardware Abstraction:** Direct3D abstracts away the complexities of different graphics hardware, allowing

developers to write code that works across a variety of GPUs.

- ○ **Rendering Pipeline:** It provides a structured pipeline for transforming 3D scenes into 2D images, handling tasks like vertex processing, rasterization, and pixel shading.
- ○ **Shader Support:** Direct3D supports programmable shaders (written in HLSL), giving developers fine-grained control over the rendering process.
- ○ **Resource Management:** It provides mechanisms for managing graphics resources like textures, buffers, and meshes.

2. Direct2D: Accelerated 2D Graphics

Direct2D is a hardware-accelerated API for rendering high-quality 2D graphics. It's designed for modern graphics hardware and offers features like:

- **High Performance:** Direct2D leverages the GPU for fast and efficient 2D rendering.
- **Anti-aliasing:** It provides smooth edges and curves for visually appealing graphics.
- **Support for Various Geometries:** Direct2D can render various shapes, paths, and text.

- **Interoperability with Direct3D:** It can seamlessly integrate with Direct3D, allowing developers to combine 2D and 3D elements in their applications.

3. DirectSound: Immersive Audio

DirectSound provides a low-level API for audio playback and capture. While it's less prominent in modern game development (often replaced by XAudio2), it still offers features like:

- **Hardware Acceleration:** DirectSound can leverage sound cards for efficient audio processing.
- **3D Sound:** It supports spatial audio, allowing developers to create immersive sound experiences where audio appears to come from specific locations in 3D space.
- **Mixing and Effects:** DirectSound provides capabilities for mixing audio streams and applying effects.

4. DirectInput: Handling User Input

DirectInput is an API for handling input from various devices, including keyboards, mice, joysticks, and gamepads. It offers features like:

- **Device Abstraction:** DirectInput provides a consistent way to access input from different devices.
- **Force Feedback:** It supports force feedback devices, allowing developers to create immersive experiences with haptic feedback.
- **Low-Level Access:** DirectInput provides low-level access to input devices, giving developers fine-grained control over input handling.

5. DirectPlay: Networking for Games

DirectPlay was an API for simplifying network communication in games. While it's been deprecated in favor of more modern networking libraries, it played a significant role in early online games.

6. Other Components:

DirectX includes several other components, such as:

- **DXGI (DirectX Graphics Infrastructure):** Handles tasks like enumerating graphics adapters, creating swap chains, and managing resources.
- **DirectWrite:** Provides a modern API for high-quality text rendering.
- **DirectCompute:** Enables general-purpose computing on the GPU.

- **XAudio2:** A low-level audio API that has largely replaced DirectSound in modern game development.
- **XACT3:** A high-level audio API built on top of XAudio2.

DirectX 12: The Modern Era

DirectX 12 is the latest major version of DirectX, offering significant improvements in performance, efficiency, and control over graphics hardware. It introduces new concepts like:

- **Explicit Resource Management:** Gives developers more direct control over GPU resources.
- **Pipeline State Objects (PSOs):** Allow for pre-configured rendering pipelines for increased efficiency.
- **Command Queues and Lists:** Enable more efficient parallel execution of graphics commands.

Moving Forward:

Understanding the various components of DirectX gives you a broader perspective on its capabilities and how it can be used to create multimedia-rich applications. In the next section, we'll delve into the graphics pipeline, which is the core process by which Direct3D transforms 3D scenes into 2D images.

The Graphics Pipeline

The graphics pipeline is the heart of real-time 3D rendering. It's a series of steps that transform 3D scene data (vertices, textures, lighting) into a 2D image displayed on your screen. Think of it as an assembly line where each stage performs a specific operation on the data, passing it along to the next stage until the final image is produced.

Here's a breakdown of the key stages in the DirectX graphics pipeline:

1. Input Assembler Stage:

- **Gathering Data:** This stage gathers the raw vertex data (positions, colors, normals, texture coordinates) from vertex buffers and index buffers.
- **Primitive Assembly:** It assembles the vertices into geometric primitives (triangles, lines, points) based on the indices provided.

2. Vertex Shader Stage:

- **Processing Vertices:** The vertex shader is a programmable stage where you can perform operations on individual vertices.
- **Transformations:** This is where you apply transformations (translation, rotation, scaling) to position vertices in the 3D world and project them onto the 2D screen.
- **Output:** The vertex shader outputs transformed vertices and any associated data (like colors or texture coordinates) to the next stage.

3. Rasterization Stage:

- **From Vertices to Pixels:** This stage converts the geometric primitives (triangles) into a set of fragments (potential pixels).
- **Interpolation:** It interpolates vertex attributes (like color and texture coordinates) across the surface of the triangle to determine the attributes of each fragment.
- **Clipping:** Fragments that fall outside the viewing frustum (the visible region of the scene) are discarded.

4. Pixel Shader Stage:

- **Processing Fragments:** The pixel shader is another programmable stage where you can perform operations on individual fragments.

- **Determining Color:** This is where you calculate the final color of each fragment based on lighting, textures, and other factors.
- **Output:** The pixel shader outputs the color and depth of each fragment.

5. Output Merger Stage:

- **Depth Testing:** This stage performs depth testing to determine which fragments are visible (closest to the viewer).
- **Blending:** It blends the colors of overlapping fragments based on transparency and other blending modes.
- **Output:** The final pixel colors are written to the render target (usually the back buffer), ready to be presented on the screen.

DirectX 12 and the Pipeline:

DirectX 12 introduces more flexibility and control over the graphics pipeline. It allows for more fine-grained management of resources and parallel execution of commands, enabling developers to optimize performance for modern hardware.

Key Concepts:

- **Shaders:** Programmable stages (vertex shader, pixel shader) that allow you to customize the rendering process.
- **Buffers:** Memory blocks on the GPU that store data like vertices, indices, and textures.
- **Render Targets:** Buffers that store the rendered image (usually the back buffer, which is swapped to the front buffer for display).
- **Pipeline State Objects (PSOs):** In DirectX 12, PSOs encapsulate the configuration of the graphics pipeline, including shader programs, blend states, and rasterizer states.

Moving Forward:

Understanding the graphics pipeline is crucial for comprehending how Direct3D transforms 3D scenes into 2D images. In the next chapter, we'll dive into the world of shaders, which are essential for customizing the rendering process and creating a wide range of visual effects.

DirectX 12 Overview

DirectX 12 marks a significant leap forward in graphics programming, offering a closer-to-the-metal approach that unlocks greater performance and efficiency on modern GPUs. It empowers developers with more control over hardware resources and enables them to create richer, more detailed, and more immersive visual experiences.

Key Features and Improvements:

1. **Reduced CPU Overhead:**
   - **Multi-threaded Command Buffer Recording:** DirectX 12 allows multiple CPU cores to record graphics commands simultaneously, reducing bottlenecks and improving efficiency.
   - **Asynchronous Compute:** It enables the GPU to perform compute tasks concurrently with graphics rendering, further maximizing hardware utilization.
2. **Enhanced Resource Management:**
   - **Explicit Control:** DirectX 12 gives developers more explicit control over GPU resources (memory, textures, buffers). This allows for finer-grained optimization and reduces driver overhead.
   - **Descriptor Heaps and Tables:** It introduces new mechanisms for managing resources, improving efficiency and reducing resource binding overhead.
3. **Pipeline State Objects (PSOs):**
   - **Pre-configured Pipelines:** PSOs encapsulate the entire rendering pipeline state (shaders, blend states, rasterizer

states, etc.). This allows for pre-compilation and reduces pipeline switching overhead, improving performance.

4. **Command Queues and Lists:**
   - **Parallel Execution:** DirectX 12 uses command queues and lists to submit graphics commands to the GPU. This enables more efficient parallel execution and better utilization of GPU resources.

5. **New Rendering Techniques:**
   - **DirectX Raytracing (DXR):** DirectX 12 introduces native support for ray tracing, a rendering technique that simulates the physical behavior of light for realistic reflections, refractions, and shadows.
   - **Variable Rate Shading (VRS):** VRS allows developers to vary the shading rate across different regions of the screen, optimizing performance by reducing the computational load in less detailed areas.
   - **Mesh Shaders:** Mesh shaders provide more flexibility in geometry processing, enabling new techniques for generating and manipulating geometry on the GPU.

Benefits of DirectX 12:

- **Increased Performance:** Reduced CPU overhead and more efficient resource management lead to significant performance gains, especially on multi-core CPUs.
- **Lower Latency:** More efficient command submission and execution result in lower input latency, making games feel more responsive.
- **Richer Visuals:** New rendering techniques like ray tracing and mesh shaders enable more realistic and detailed graphics.
- **Greater Control:** DirectX 12 provides developers with more control over hardware resources and the rendering process, allowing for deeper optimization.

Challenges of DirectX 12:

- **Increased Complexity:** The closer-to-the-metal approach of DirectX 12 requires a deeper understanding of graphics hardware and more explicit resource management.
- **Steeper Learning Curve:** Mastering the new concepts and techniques in DirectX 12 can be more challenging for beginners.

Moving Forward:

DirectX 12 represents the future of graphics programming on Windows. While it presents some challenges, the performance benefits and new rendering capabilities make it an exciting API to learn and explore. In the upcoming chapters, we'll delve into the specifics of DirectX 12 programming, covering key concepts like resource management, command lists, and shaders.

Key DirectX Concepts (Resources, Descriptors, Pipelines)

DirectX 12 introduces several key concepts that are crucial for understanding its inner workings and efficiently utilizing the graphics hardware. Let's explore three fundamental concepts: resources, descriptors, and pipelines.

1. Resources: The Building Blocks

Resources are the fundamental data structures in DirectX 12. They represent various types of data that the GPU can access and manipulate, including:

- **Textures:** Store image data used for texture mapping, rendering targets, and other purposes.
- **Buffers:** Hold structured or unstructured data, such as vertex data, index data, constant buffers, and more.
- **Depth-Stencil Buffers:** Store depth and stencil information used for depth testing and stencil operations.

Key characteristics of resources:

- **GPU Memory:** Resources reside in GPU memory, allowing for fast access by the graphics hardware.
- **Typed:** Each resource has a specific type (texture, buffer, etc.) and format (e.g., R8G8B8A8 for a 32-bit color texture).
- **States:** Resources can have different states (e.g., render target, shader resource, unordered access) that determine how they can be used.

2. Descriptors: Describing Resources

Descriptors are small data structures that describe resources to the GPU. They act as intermediaries between your application code and the GPU, providing the necessary information for the hardware to access and utilize resources correctly.

Types of descriptors:

- **Shader Resource View (SRV):** Allows a shader to read data from a resource (e.g., sampling a texture).
- **Unordered Access View (UAV):** Allows a shader to read and write data to a resource (e.g., writing to a texture).
- **Constant Buffer View (CBV):** Allows a shader to access data in a constant buffer.

- **Sampler:** Defines how texture data is sampled (e.g., filtering, addressing modes).
- **Render Target View (RTV):** Specifies a resource as a render target (where the rendered image is written).
- **Depth Stencil View (DSV):** Specifies a resource as a depth-stencil buffer.

Descriptor Heaps and Tables:

- **Descriptor Heaps:** Descriptors are allocated from descriptor heaps, which are blocks of memory on the GPU that store sets of descriptors.
- **Descriptor Tables:** Descriptors can be organized into descriptor tables, which are contiguous ranges within a descriptor heap.

3. Pipelines: Defining the Rendering Process

Pipelines define the sequence of operations that the GPU performs to render a scene. They encapsulate various stages of the graphics pipeline and their configurations.

Types of pipelines:

- **Graphics Pipeline:** Used for rendering 3D graphics. It includes stages like vertex shading, rasterization, and pixel shading.

- **Compute Pipeline:** Used for general-purpose computing on the GPU.

Pipeline State Objects (PSOs):

- **Encapsulating Pipeline State:** PSOs are objects that store the entire state of a pipeline, including:
  - **Shaders:** The programs that run on the vertex and pixel shader stages.
  - **Input Layout:** Describes the format of vertex data.
  - **Rasterizer State:** Controls how primitives are rasterized (e.g., fill mode, cull mode).
  - **Blend State:** Defines how colors are blended.
  - **Depth-Stencil State:** Configures depth and stencil testing.

Why these concepts are important:

- **Efficiency:** Descriptors and PSOs allow for efficient resource binding and pipeline switching, reducing overhead and improving performance.
- **Flexibility:** DirectX 12's explicit resource management and pipeline configuration provide greater flexibility and control over the rendering process.
- **Modern Hardware:** These concepts are designed to take advantage of modern GPU

architectures, enabling developers to maximize hardware utilization.

Moving Forward:

Understanding resources, descriptors, and pipelines is fundamental to working with DirectX 12. In the upcoming chapters, we'll dive deeper into how to create and manage these objects, write shaders, and build complete rendering pipelines.

Hello, DirectX! (Your First Triangle)

It's time to put theory into practice and create your first DirectX 12 program! This classic "Hello, World!" of graphics programming will guide you through the essential steps of setting up a basic DirectX 12 application and rendering a simple triangle on the screen.

1. Project Setup:

- **Create a New Project:** In Visual Studio, create a new "Windows Desktop Application" project (as described in Chapter 1).
- **Include Headers and Link Libraries:** Make sure to include the necessary DirectX 12 headers (d3d12.h, dxgi1_4.h) and link the required libraries (d3d12.lib, dxgi.lib, d3dcompiler.lib).

2. Initialization:

- **Enable Debugging:** Enable the debug layer during development to catch errors and receive helpful messages.
- **Create the Device:** Create a ID3D12Device object, which represents the graphics adapter.
- **Create the Command Queue:** Create a ID3D12CommandQueue to submit commands to the GPU.
- **Create the Swap Chain:** Create a IDXGISwapChain3 to manage the presentation of rendered frames to the screen.
- **Create Descriptor Heaps:** Create descriptor heaps for render target views (RTVs) and depth stencil views (DSVs).
- **Create Command Allocators:** Create command allocators to allocate memory for command lists.
- **Create Command Lists:** Create ID3D12GraphicsCommandList objects to record graphics commands.
- **Create Fence:** Create a fence to synchronize CPU and GPU operations.

3. Resource Creation:

- **Create Render Target:** Create a texture resource to serve as the render target (where the rendered image will be stored).
- **Create Depth Stencil Buffer:** Create a texture resource to serve as the depth-stencil buffer.

- **Create Vertex Buffer:** Create a buffer resource to store the vertex data for the triangle.
- **Create Root Signature:** Create a root signature to define the input resources for the shaders.
- **Compile Shaders:** Compile the vertex shader and pixel shader code (written in HLSL) into bytecode.
- **Create Pipeline State Object (PSO):** Create a PSO that encapsulates the pipeline configuration, including the shaders, input layout, and other states.

4. Rendering:

- **Populate Vertex Buffer:** Fill the vertex buffer with the coordinates of the triangle's vertices.
- **Record Commands:** Record the rendering commands into the command list:
    - **Set Pipeline State:** Set the PSO to configure the pipeline.
    - **Set Root Signature:** Set the root signature to define input resources.
    - **Set Viewport and Scissor Rect:** Define the area of the render target to render to.
    - **Set Render Targets:** Bind the render target and depth-stencil buffer.
    - **Clear Render Targets:** Clear the render target and depth-stencil buffer to a specific color.

- ○ **Set Vertex Buffer:** Bind the vertex buffer.
  - ○ **Draw:** Issue a draw call to render the triangle.
- **Execute Command List:** Submit the command list to the command queue for execution.
- **Present Frame:** Present the rendered frame to the screen by swapping the back buffer with the front buffer.

5. Cleanup:

- **Wait for GPU:** Wait for the GPU to finish executing the commands.
- **Release Resources:** Release all DirectX resources (device, command queue, swap chain, etc.) when the application exits.

Code Example (Simplified):

C++

```
// ... (Initialization and resource creation) ...


// Record commands

commandList->IASetPrimitiveTopology(D3D_PRIMITI
VE_TOPOLOGY_TRIANGLELIST);
```

```cpp
commandList->SetGraphicsRootSignature(rootSignature
.Get());

commandList->RSSetViewports(1, &viewport);

commandList->RSSetScissorRects(1, &scissorRect);


commandList->ResourceBarrier(1,
&CD3DX12_RESOURCE_BARRIER::Transition(rende
rTargets[frameIndex].Get(),
D3D12_RESOURCE_STATE_PRESENT,
D3D12_RESOURCE_STATE_RENDER_TARGET));


CD3DX12_CPU_DESCRIPTOR_HANDLE
rtvHandle(rtvHeap->GetCPUDescriptorHandleForHeap
Start(), frameIndex, rtvDescriptorSize);

CD3DX12_CPU_DESCRIPTOR_HANDLE
dsvHandle(dsvHeap->GetCPUDescriptorHandleForHea
pStart());

commandList->OMSetRenderTargets(1,      &rtvHandle,
FALSE, &dsvHandle);


const float clearColor[] = { 0.0f, 0.2f, 0.4f, 1.0f };
```

```cpp
commandList->ClearRenderTargetView(rtvHandle,
clearColor, 0, nullptr);

commandList->ClearDepthStencilView(dsvHandle,
D3D12_CLEAR_FLAG_DEPTH, 1.0f, 0, 0, nullptr);


commandList->IASetVertexBuffers(0,                    1,
&vertexBufferView);

commandList->DrawInstanced(3, 1, 0, 0);


commandList->ResourceBarrier(1,
&CD3DX12_RESOURCE_BARRIER::Transition(rende
rTargets[frameIndex].Get(),
D3D12_RESOURCE_STATE_RENDER_TARGET,
D3D12_RESOURCE_STATE_PRESENT));


commandList->Close();


// Execute command list and present frame

// ...
```

Congratulations! You've rendered your first triangle with DirectX 12. This is a significant step in your graphics programming journey. As you progress through this book, you'll build upon this foundation to create more complex and exciting 3D scenes.

Chapter 4: Working with Shaders

What are Shaders? (Vertex Shaders, Pixel Shaders)

Shaders are small programs that run on the Graphics Processing Unit (GPU). They give you, the developer, incredible control over the rendering process, allowing you to create a wide range of visual effects and customize how objects appear on the screen. Think of them as mini-programs that manipulate graphics data at various stages of the rendering pipeline.

Why Shaders are Essential

Before shaders, graphics cards had fixed-function pipelines, limiting the visual effects you could achieve. Shaders introduced programmability, allowing you to define custom algorithms for processing vertices and pixels, leading to:

- **Realism:** Shaders enable realistic lighting, shadows, and surface details.
- **Special Effects:** You can create a vast array of special effects like fire, smoke, water, and more.
- **Customization:** Shaders give you fine-grained control over the appearance of objects and scenes.

- **Performance:** Shaders leverage the parallel processing power of the GPU, enabling efficient rendering of complex effects.

Types of Shaders

In DirectX, we primarily work with two main types of shaders:

1. Vertex Shaders

- **Purpose:** Vertex shaders operate on individual vertices of a 3D model. They are responsible for:
    - **Transforming Vertices:** Positioning vertices in the 3D world and projecting them onto the 2D screen.
    - **Calculating Lighting:** Determining how light interacts with each vertex.
    - **Passing Data:** Passing data (like color or texture coordinates) to the pixel shader.
- **Input:** Vertex shaders receive data about each vertex, including:
    - **Position:** The 3D coordinates of the vertex.
    - **Normal:** A vector perpendicular to the surface at the vertex, used for lighting calculations.
    - **Texture Coordinates:** Coordinates that map the vertex to a point on a texture.

- ○ **Color:** The color of the vertex.
- **Output:** Vertex shaders output the transformed vertex position and any associated data to the next stage in the pipeline.

2. Pixel Shaders

- **Purpose:** Pixel shaders (also known as fragment shaders) operate on individual pixels (or fragments) of a rendered image. They are responsible for:
  - ○ **Calculating Color:** Determining the final color of each pixel based on lighting, textures, and other factors.
  - ○ **Applying Effects:** Creating special effects like shadows, reflections, and post-processing effects.
- **Input:** Pixel shaders receive interpolated data from the vertex shader, including:
  - ○ **Interpolated Vertex Attributes:** Position, normal, texture coordinates, and color, interpolated across the surface of the triangle.
  - ○ **Texture Data:** Color information from textures sampled based on texture coordinates.
- **Output:** Pixel shaders output the final color and depth of each pixel.

The Shader Pipeline

Vertex shaders and pixel shaders work together in the graphics pipeline:

1. **Vertex Processing:** The vertex shader processes each vertex of a 3D model.
2. **Rasterization:** The rasterizer converts the processed vertices into fragments.
3. **Pixel Processing:** The pixel shader processes each fragment to determine its final color.

Writing Shaders

Shaders are written in a special language called HLSL (High-Level Shading Language), which is similar to C++. HLSL provides features specifically designed for graphics programming, including:

- **Vector and Matrix Types:** Built-in support for vectors and matrices, essential for graphics calculations.
- **Texture Sampling:** Functions for accessing and sampling textures.
- **Lighting Functions:** Functions for calculating lighting effects.

Example Shader Code (HLSL):

High-level shader language

```
// Vertex Shader
struct VS_INPUT
{
    float3 position : POSITION;
    float2 texcoord : TEXCOORD;
};

struct VS_OUTPUT
{
    float4 position : SV_POSITION;
    float2 texcoord : TEXCOORD;
};

VS_OUTPUT main(VS_INPUT input)
{
    VS_OUTPUT output;

    output.position = float4(input.position, 1.0f); // Transform to homogeneous coordinates
```

```
    output.texcoord = input.texcoord;

    return output;

}


// Pixel Shader

Texture2D texture0 : register(t0);

SamplerState sampler0 : register(s0);


float4 main(VS_OUTPUT input) : SV_TARGET

{

    return texture0.Sample(sampler0, input.texcoord); // Sample the texture

}
```

Moving Forward:

Shaders are the key to creating stunning and dynamic visuals in your DirectX applications. In the next section, we'll delve deeper into HLSL, exploring its syntax, data types, and functions, and learn how to write your own shaders to customize the rendering process.

HLSL (High-Level Shading Language) Basics

HLSL (High-Level Shading Language) is the programming language you'll use to write shaders in DirectX. It's similar to C++ in syntax and structure, but with added features and data types specifically designed for graphics programming. Let's explore the basics of HLSL to get you started with writing your own shaders.

1. Structure of an HLSL Shader

An HLSL shader typically consists of:

- **Input and Output Structures:** Define the data that the shader receives as input and the data it produces as output.
- **Variables:** Declare variables to store data within the shader.
- **Functions:** Define functions to perform specific operations.
- **Entry Point Function:** The main function is the entry point where the shader execution begins.

Example:

High-level shader language

```
struct VS_INPUT
{
```

```
    float3 position : POSITION;

    float2 texcoord : TEXCOORD;

};


struct VS_OUTPUT

{

    float4 position : SV_POSITION;

    float2 texcoord : TEXCOORD;

};


VS_OUTPUT main(VS_INPUT input)

{

    VS_OUTPUT output;

    // ... shader code ...

    return output;

}
```

2. Data Types

HLSL provides various data types, including:

- **Scalar Types:**
  - bool: Boolean value (true or false).
  - int: Integer.
  - float: Floating-point number.
  - double: Double-precision floating-point number.
- **Vector Types:**
  - float2: 2D vector of floats.
  - float3: 3D vector of floats.
  - float4: 4D vector of floats (often used for homogeneous coordinates).
- **Matrix Types:**
  - float4x4: 4x4 matrix of floats.
- **Texture Types:**
  - Texture2D: 2D texture.
  - Texture3D: 3D texture.
  - TextureCube: Cubemap texture.
- **Sampler Types:**
  - SamplerState: Defines how texture data is sampled.

3. Operators

HLSL supports standard C++ operators, including:

- **Arithmetic Operators:** +, -, *, /, %
- **Comparison Operators:** ==, !=, >, <, >=, <=

- **Logical Operators:** &&, ||, !
- **Bitwise Operators:** &, |, ^, ~, <<, >>
- **Assignment Operators:** =, +=, -=, *=, /=, %=

4. Control Flow Statements

HLSL supports control flow statements similar to C++:

- **Conditional Statements:** if, else if, else
- **Loops:** for, while, do-while

5. Functions

You can define functions in HLSL to encapsulate reusable code:

High-level shader language

```
float3 calculateLight(float3 normal, float3 lightDir)

{

    // ... lighting calculation ...

}
```

6. Built-in Functions

HLSL provides a rich set of built-in functions for common graphics operations:

- **Math Functions:** abs, sin, cos, tan, pow, sqrt, etc.
- **Texture Sampling:** texture.Sample, texture.Load
- **Geometric Functions:** dot, cross, normalize, length, distance
- **Clipping Functions:** clip

7. Semantics

Semantics are keywords that provide additional information about variables in HLSL. They are used to:

- **Link Shader Inputs and Outputs:** Connect variables between shader stages (e.g., POSITION for vertex position, SV_POSITION for output position).
- **Identify System-Value Semantics:** Access special system values (e.g., SV_TARGET for the pixel shader output).

Example:

High-level shader language

```
float4 main(VS_OUTPUT input) : SV_TARGET
{
    // ... shader code ...
}
```

Moving Forward:

With a grasp of these HLSL basics, you're ready to start writing your own shaders. In the next section, we'll explore shader compilation and linking, and learn how to integrate your shaders into your DirectX 12 applications.

Shader Compilation and Linking

Before your shaders can be used by the graphics pipeline, they need to be compiled from HLSL source code into a format that the GPU can understand. This process involves compilation and, optionally, linking.

1. Shader Compilation

- **HLSL Compiler:** DirectX provides an HLSL compiler (D3DCompileFromFile) that takes your HLSL source code and converts it into bytecode. This bytecode is a low-level representation of your shader that the GPU can execute.
- **Compilation Flags:** You can specify various compilation flags to control the compilation process, such as:
    - **Optimization Level:** Control the level of optimization performed by the compiler.

- ○ **Target Profile:** Specify the shader model (e.g., vs_5_0 for vertex shader model 5.0) to target specific GPU capabilities.
- ○ **Debugging Information:** Include debugging information in the compiled bytecode to aid in shader debugging.

Example (Compiling a shader from a file):

```cpp
C++

ID3DBlob* vertexShaderBlob;

D3DCompileFromFile(L"vertexShader.hlsl", nullptr, nullptr, "main", "vs_5_0", 0, 0, &vertexShaderBlob, nullptr);
```

2. Shader Linking (Optional)

- **Combining Shaders:** Shader linking allows you to combine multiple shader stages (e.g., vertex shader and pixel shader) into a single program. This can be useful for:
  - ○ **Sharing Data:** Allows shaders to share variables and constants.
  - ○ **Optimization:** The compiler can perform optimizations across shader stages.

- **Linking Process:** The HLSL compiler can also perform shader linking. You provide the compiled bytecode of the individual shaders, and it produces a linked shader program.

3. Creating Pipeline State Objects (PSOs)

- **Incorporating Shaders:** Once your shaders are compiled (and optionally linked), you incorporate them into a Pipeline State Object (PSO). The PSO encapsulates the entire pipeline configuration, including the shaders, input layout, rasterizer state, blend state, and depth-stencil state.
- **Creating the PSO:** You use the ID3D12Device::CreateGraphicsPipelineState function to create a PSO, providing the compiled shader bytecode and other pipeline state configurations.

Example (Creating a PSO with compiled shaders):

C++

```
D3D12_GRAPHICS_PIPELINE_STATE_DESC
psoDesc = {};

psoDesc.VS = {
reinterpret_cast<BYTE*>(vertexShaderBlob->GetBuffer
Pointer()), vertexShaderBlob->GetBufferSize() };
```

```
psoDesc.PS                    =                    {
reinterpret_cast<BYTE*>(pixelShaderBlob->GetBuffer
Pointer()), pixelShaderBlob->GetBufferSize() };

// ... (other PSO configurations) ...


ID3D12PipelineState* pipelineState;

device->CreateGraphicsPipelineState(&psoDesc,
IID_PPV_ARGS(&pipelineState));
```

Best Practices

- **Compile Offline:** Compile your shaders offline
  whenever possible. Shader compilation can be
  time-consuming, so doing it offline avoids
  performance hiccups during runtime.
- **Error Handling:** Implement proper error
  handling during shader compilation and linking
  to catch any issues with your HLSL code.
- **Optimization:** Use appropriate compilation flags
  to optimize your shaders for performance.
- **Shader Reflection:** Consider using shader
  reflection to retrieve information about the input
  and output variables of your shaders. This can be
  useful for dynamically setting up resource
  bindings.

Moving Forward:

With your shaders compiled and linked, you're ready to integrate them into your DirectX 12 applications. In the next chapter, we'll explore how to use shaders to draw various primitives and create basic 3D scenes.

Data Communication Between CPU and GPU

In DirectX 12, efficient data communication between the CPU and the GPU is crucial for achieving high performance. The CPU is responsible for preparing and submitting rendering commands and data to the GPU, while the GPU executes those commands and processes the data to render the final image. Let's explore how this communication takes place.

1. Uploading Data to the GPU

- **Resources:** Data that the GPU needs to access (vertices, indices, textures, constant buffers) is stored in resources. These resources reside in GPU memory for fast access by the graphics hardware.
- **Uploading:** To get data from the CPU's memory to the GPU's memory, you typically:
    - **Create a Resource:** Create a resource of the appropriate type (buffer, texture) and size.

- ○ **Map the Resource:** Map the resource into the CPU's address space, allowing the CPU to write data directly into the resource's memory.
- ○ **Copy Data:** Copy the data from the CPU's memory to the mapped resource memory.
- ○ **Unmap the Resource:** Unmap the resource to make it accessible to the GPU.

Example (Uploading vertex data to a buffer):

C++

```
// Create a vertex buffer resource

ID3D12Resource* vertexBuffer;

device->CreateCommittedResource(

    // ... (resource description) ...

    IID_PPV_ARGS(&vertexBuffer));


// Map the vertex buffer

void* vertexData;

vertexBuffer->Map(0, nullptr, &vertexData);
```

```
// Copy vertex data to the buffer

memcpy(vertexData, vertices, sizeof(vertices));


// Unmap the vertex buffer

vertexBuffer->Unmap(0, nullptr);
```

2. Constant Buffers

- **Dynamic Data:** Constant buffers are used to pass frequently changing data to the GPU, such as world matrices, view matrices, projection matrices, and lighting parameters.
- **Updating:** To update a constant buffer:
  - **Map the Constant Buffer:** Map the constant buffer resource into the CPU's address space.
  - **Update Data:** Write the new data into the mapped memory.
  - **Unmap the Constant Buffer:** Unmap the resource.

3. Resource Barriers

- **State Transitions:** Resources can be in different states (e.g., render target, shader resource, copy source, copy destination). You use resource barriers to transition resources between states.

- **Synchronization:** Resource barriers also help synchronize access to resources between the CPU and the GPU.

Example (Transitioning a resource from copy destination to vertex buffer):

C++

```
commandList->ResourceBarrier(1,
&CD3DX12_RESOURCE_BARRIER::Transition(verte
xBuffer.Get(),
D3D12_RESOURCE_STATE_COPY_DEST,
D3D12_RESOURCE_STATE_VERTEX_AND_CONST
ANT_BUFFER));
```

4. Command Lists and Queues

- **Recording Commands:** The CPU records rendering commands (draw calls, resource binding, state changes) into command lists.
- **Submitting Commands:** Command lists are submitted to command queues for execution by the GPU.
- **Synchronization:** Fences are used to synchronize command execution and ensure that

the CPU doesn't submit new commands to a command queue until the GPU has finished executing previous commands.

5. Memory Management

- **GPU Memory:** Efficiently managing GPU memory is crucial for performance.
- **Memory Allocation:** DirectX 12 provides functions for allocating GPU memory and creating resources.
- **Memory Residency:** You can control the residency of resources in GPU memory to optimize memory usage.

Best Practices

- **Minimize Data Transfers:** Reduce the amount of data transferred between the CPU and GPU to minimize overhead.
- **Batch Commands:** Batch rendering commands together to reduce the number of submissions to the command queue.
- **Asynchronous Operations:** Use asynchronous compute and other techniques to overlap CPU and GPU operations.
- **Memory Alignment:** Align memory allocations to optimize data access by the GPU.

Moving Forward:

Understanding how data communication works between the CPU and GPU is crucial for writing efficient DirectX 12 applications. In the following chapters, we'll explore how to use these techniques to render various types of geometry, apply textures, and implement lighting effects.

Part II: Rendering Techniques

Chapter 5: Drawing Primitives

Vertices and Indices

In the world of 3D graphics, everything you see on the screen is constructed from basic building blocks called primitives. These primitives, such as triangles, lines, and points, are defined by their vertices and, optionally, organized using indices. Let's delve into these fundamental concepts:

1. Vertices: Defining Points in Space

A vertex is a single point in 3D space. It's more than just a coordinate; it carries information that describes its properties and how it contributes to the rendered image.

Vertex Data:

- **Position:** The fundamental attribute of a vertex, specifying its location in 3D space using (x, y, z) coordinates.
- **Color:** Defines the color of the vertex, often represented using RGB or RGBA values.
- **Normal:** A vector perpendicular to the surface at the vertex, used for lighting calculations.

- **Texture Coordinates:** Coordinates that map the vertex to a specific point on a texture image, enabling texture mapping.
- **Other Attributes:** Vertices can hold additional data, such as tangent vectors (for advanced lighting), blend weights (for animation), and more.

Vertex Structure:

You typically define a vertex structure in your code to organize the vertex data. This structure acts as a blueprint for how vertex data is stored and accessed.

C++

```
struct Vertex
{
    XMFLOAT3 position;
    XMFLOAT4 color;
    XMFLOAT3 normal;
    XMFLOAT2 texcoord;
};
```

2. Indices: Efficient Organization

Indices are optional but highly beneficial for efficiently representing 3D models. They allow you to reuse vertices, reducing data redundancy and improving rendering performance.

How Indices Work:

Instead of repeating vertex data for every triangle in a mesh, you store the vertices in a vertex buffer and use indices to define the order in which these vertices are connected to form triangles.

Example:

Consider a square made of two triangles:

```
1-----2

/\  /\

0---3 0---3
```

Without indices, you would need to define 6 vertices (2 triangles x 3 vertices each). With indices, you only need 4 vertices and 6 indices:

- **Vertices:** {0, 1, 2, 3}

- **Indices:** {0, 1, 3, 1, 2, 3}

Benefits of Using Indices:

- **Reduced Memory Usage:** Avoids redundant vertex data, especially in complex models with many shared vertices.
- **Improved Cache Efficiency:** Increases the likelihood of relevant vertex data being in the GPU's cache, improving performance.
- **Simplified Mesh Manipulation:** Makes operations like mesh deformation and animation easier.

3. Vertex and Index Buffers

- **Vertex Buffer:** A memory block on the GPU that stores vertex data.
- **Index Buffer:** A memory block on the GPU that stores indices.
- **Binding Buffers:** You bind vertex and index buffers to the rendering pipeline to make the vertex data accessible to the shaders.

4. Drawing Primitives

- **Primitive Topology:** Specifies the type of primitives to be drawn (triangles, lines, points).
- **Draw Calls:** You issue draw calls to instruct the GPU to render the primitives defined by the vertex and index buffers.

Example (Drawing a triangle list):

C++

```cpp
commandList->IASetPrimitiveTopology(D3D_PRIMITIVE_TOPOLOGY_TRIANGLELIST);

commandList->IASetVertexBuffers(0, 1, &vertexBufferView);

commandList->IASetIndexBuffer(&indexBufferView);

commandList->DrawIndexedInstanced(numIndices, 1, 0, 0, 0);
```

Moving Forward:

Understanding vertices and indices is fundamental for working with 3D geometry in DirectX. In the following sections, we'll explore how to create and populate vertex and index buffers, draw various types of primitives, and build more complex 3D models.

Vertex Buffers and Index Buffers

Vertex buffers and index buffers are essential components in DirectX for storing and managing the geometric data of your 3D models. They reside in GPU memory, allowing for efficient access and processing by the graphics hardware. Let's explore how to create and utilize these buffers in your DirectX 12 applications.

1. Creating Vertex Buffers

To create a vertex buffer, you'll need to:

- **Determine Buffer Size:** Calculate the total size of the vertex data you want to store. This is typically the size of your vertex structure multiplied by the number of vertices.
- **Create a Committed Resource:** Use the ID3D12Device::CreateCommittedResource function to allocate memory on the GPU and create a buffer resource. Specify the buffer size, heap type (default heap for static data, upload heap for dynamic data), and resource states.
- **Populate the Buffer:** Upload your vertex data to the buffer. This usually involves mapping the buffer into CPU address space, copying the data, and then unmapping it.

Example:

C++

```
// Create a vertex buffer

ID3D12Resource* vertexBuffer;

device->CreateCommittedResource(
```

```cpp
    &CD3DX12_HEAP_PROPERTIES(D3D12_HEAP_TY
PE_DEFAULT), // Default heap

    D3D12_HEAP_FLAG_NONE,

    &CD3DX12_RESOURCE_DESC::Buffer(vertexBuffer
Size),

    D3D12_RESOURCE_STATE_COPY_DEST, // Initial
state

    nullptr,

    IID_PPV_ARGS(&vertexBuffer));


// Upload heap for uploading vertex data

ID3D12Resource* vertexBufferUploadHeap;

device->CreateCommittedResource(


    &CD3DX12_HEAP_PROPERTIES(D3D12_HEAP_TY
PE_UPLOAD), // Upload heap

    D3D12_HEAP_FLAG_NONE,
```

```cpp
    &CD3DX12_RESOURCE_DESC::Buffer(vertexBuffer
Size),

    D3D12_RESOURCE_STATE_GENERIC_READ,

    nullptr,

    IID_PPV_ARGS(&vertexBufferUploadHeap));


// Map the upload heap and copy vertex data

D3D12_SUBRESOURCE_DATA vertexData = {};

vertexData.pData = vertices;

vertexData.RowPitch = vertexBufferSize;

vertexData.SlicePitch = vertexBufferSize;


UpdateSubresources(commandList.Get(),
vertexBuffer.Get(), vertexBufferUploadHeap.Get(), 0, 0,
1, &vertexData);


// Transition the vertex buffer to the correct state

commandList->ResourceBarrier(1,
&CD3DX12_RESOURCE_BARRIER::Transition(verte
```

```
xBuffer.Get(),
D3D12_RESOURCE_STATE_COPY_DEST,
D3D12_RESOURCE_STATE_VERTEX_AND_CONST
ANT_BUFFER));
```

2. Creating Index Buffers

Creating an index buffer is similar to creating a vertex buffer:

- **Determine Buffer Size:** Calculate the size of the index buffer based on the number of indices and the size of the index data type (usually 16-bit or 32-bit integers).
- **Create a Committed Resource:** Use ID3D12Device::CreateCommittedResource to allocate memory and create the index buffer resource.
- **Populate the Buffer:** Upload your index data to the buffer.

Example:

C++

```
// Create an index buffer

ID3D12Resource* indexBuffer;
```

```cpp
device->CreateCommittedResource(

&CD3DX12_HEAP_PROPERTIES(D3D12_HEAP_TYPE_DEFAULT), // Default heap
    D3D12_HEAP_FLAG_NONE,

&CD3DX12_RESOURCE_DESC::Buffer(indexBufferSize),
    D3D12_RESOURCE_STATE_COPY_DEST, // Initial state
    nullptr,
    IID_PPV_ARGS(&indexBuffer));

// Upload heap for uploading index data
ID3D12Resource* indexBufferUploadHeap;
device->CreateCommittedResource(

&CD3DX12_HEAP_PROPERTIES(D3D12_HEAP_TYPE_UPLOAD), // Upload heap
    D3D12_HEAP_FLAG_NONE,
```

```cpp
        &CD3DX12_RESOURCE_DESC::Buffer(indexBufferSize),

            D3D12_RESOURCE_STATE_GENERIC_READ,

            nullptr,

            IID_PPV_ARGS(&indexBufferUploadHeap));


        // Map the upload heap and copy index data

        D3D12_SUBRESOURCE_DATA indexData = {};

        indexData.pData = indices;

        indexData.RowPitch = indexBufferSize;

        indexData.SlicePitch = indexBufferSize;


        UpdateSubresources(commandList.Get(),
        indexBuffer.Get(), indexBufferUploadHeap.Get(), 0, 0,
        1, &indexData);


        // Transition the index buffer to the correct state

        commandList->ResourceBarrier(1,
        &CD3DX12_RESOURCE_BARRIER::Transition(index
```

```
Buffer.Get(),
D3D12_RESOURCE_STATE_COPY_DEST,
D3D12_RESOURCE_STATE_INDEX_BUFFER));
```

3. Binding Vertex and Index Buffers

Before you can draw your geometry, you need to bind the vertex and index buffers to the rendering pipeline:

- **Create Views:** Create D3D12_VERTEX_BUFFER_VIEW and D3D12_INDEX_BUFFER_VIEW structures to describe the buffers.
- **Set Vertex Buffers:** Use the ID3D12GraphicsCommandList::IASetVertexBuffers function to bind the vertex buffer(s).
- **Set Index Buffer:** Use the ID3D12GraphicsCommandList::IASetIndexBuffer function to bind the index buffer.

Example:

C++

// Create vertex buffer view

```
D3D12_VERTEX_BUFFER_VIEW vertexBufferView
= {};
```

```cpp
vertexBufferView.BufferLocation                =
vertexBuffer->GetGPUVirtualAddress();

vertexBufferView.StrideInBytes = sizeof(Vertex);

vertexBufferView.SizeInBytes = vertexBufferSize;


// Create index buffer view

D3D12_INDEX_BUFFER_VIEW   indexBufferView  =
{};

indexBufferView.BufferLocation                =
indexBuffer->GetGPUVirtualAddress();

indexBufferView.Format                        =
DXGI_FORMAT_R16_UINT; // 16-bit indices

indexBufferView.SizeInBytes = indexBufferSize;


// Bind the vertex and index buffers

commandList->IASetVertexBuffers(0,            1,
&vertexBufferView);

commandList->IASetIndexBuffer(&indexBufferView);
```

4. Drawing with Buffers

Once the buffers are bound, you can issue draw calls to render your geometry. You specify the primitive topology (e.g., triangle list) and the number of vertices or indices to draw.

Example:

C++

```
commandList->IASetPrimitiveTopology(D3D_PRIMITI
VE_TOPOLOGY_TRIANGLELIST);

commandList->DrawIndexedInstanced(numIndices, 1, 0,
0, 0); // Draw indexed geometry
```

Moving Forward:

With a solid understanding of vertex and index buffers, you can efficiently store and manage the geometric data of your 3D models in DirectX 12. In the next section, we'll explore how to draw various types of primitives and build more complex 3D scenes.

Rendering Triangles, Lines, and Points

In DirectX, you can render various types of primitives, but the most common ones are triangles, lines, and points. These primitives form the foundation for representing and rendering 3D objects and scenes. Let's explore how to render each of these primitives.

1. Rendering Triangles

Triangles are the most fundamental primitive in 3D graphics. They are used to construct meshes, which are collections of triangles that form the surfaces of 3D objects.

- **Triangle List:** The most common way to render triangles is using a triangle list. In this mode, every three vertices define a separate triangle.
- **Triangle Strip:** A triangle strip is a more efficient way to render a sequence of connected triangles. Each new vertex, after the first two, defines a new triangle using the previous two vertices.
- **Triangle Fan:** A triangle fan is similar to a triangle strip, but each new vertex forms a triangle with the first vertex and the previous vertex.

Example (Rendering a triangle list):

C++

```
// Set the primitive topology
```

```cpp
commandList->IASetPrimitiveTopology(D3D_PRIMITI
VE_TOPOLOGY_TRIANGLELIST);


// Draw the triangles

commandList->DrawIndexedInstanced(numIndices, 1, 0,
0, 0);
```

2. Rendering Lines

Lines are used to render wireframe models, outlines, and other line-based graphics.

- **Line List:** Each pair of vertices defines a separate line segment.
- **Line Strip:** A sequence of connected line segments. Each new vertex, after the first, defines a new line segment with the previous vertex.

Example (Rendering a line list):

C++

```cpp
// Set the primitive topology

commandList->IASetPrimitiveTopology(D3D_PRIMITI
VE_TOPOLOGY_LINELIST);
```

// Draw the lines

```
commandList->DrawIndexedInstanced(numIndices, 1, 0,
0, 0);
```

3. Rendering Points

Points are used to render particle effects, point clouds, and other effects where individual points are visualized.

- **Point List:** Each vertex defines a single point.

Example (Rendering a point list):

C++

```
// Set the primitive topology
commandList->IASetPrimitiveTopology(D3D_PRIMITI
VE_TOPOLOGY_POINTLIST);


// Draw the points
commandList->DrawIndexedInstanced(numVertices, 1,
0, 0, 0);
```

Choosing the Right Primitive Topology

The choice of primitive topology depends on the type of geometry you want to render and the structure of your vertex data. Triangle lists are the most general-purpose, while triangle strips and fans can be more efficient for certain types of meshes.

Important Considerations

- **Winding Order:** The order in which you define the vertices of a triangle (clockwise or counter-clockwise) determines its winding order. This is important for backface culling, which optimizes rendering by discarding triangles facing away from the camera.
- **Vertex Order:** For line strips and triangle strips, the order of vertices affects how the lines and triangles are connected.
- **Performance:** Using the appropriate primitive topology can improve rendering performance by reducing the amount of data that needs to be processed.

Moving Forward:

With the ability to render triangles, lines, and points, you have the tools to create a wide variety of 3D graphics. In the next section, we'll explore how to introduce 3D models into your DirectX applications, allowing you to render more complex and interesting objects.

Introducing 3D Models

While rendering individual primitives like triangles, lines, and points is essential, the real magic of 3D graphics lies in bringing complex 3D models to life. These models, often created in external 3D modeling software, represent objects with intricate shapes, textures, and details. Let's explore how to introduce these 3D models into your DirectX applications.

1. 3D Model Formats

3D models are typically stored in various file formats that encapsulate the model's geometry, materials, and other attributes. Some common formats include:

- **.obj (Wavefront OBJ):** A simple text-based format that stores vertex positions, normals, texture coordinates, and face definitions.
- **.fbx (Autodesk FBX):** A more versatile format that can store animation data, skeletal information, and other complex attributes.
- **.glTF (GL Transmission Format):** A modern, web-friendly format designed for efficient transmission and rendering of 3D models.

- **.dae (COLLADA):** An XML-based format that aims to be an interchange format for various 3D applications.

2. Loading 3D Models

DirectX doesn't provide built-in functions for loading 3D models directly from these file formats. You'll typically need to use a third-party library or write your own code to parse the model file and extract the necessary data.

Popular Libraries:

- **Assimp (Open Asset Import Library):** A powerful library that supports a wide range of 3D model formats. It handles parsing the file, loading the data, and converting it into a format suitable for use in DirectX.
- **TinyObjLoader:** A lightweight, single-header library for loading .obj files.
- **DirectXMesh:** A library from Microsoft that provides helper functions for loading and processing meshes.

3. Extracting Model Data

Once you've loaded the 3D model, you'll need to extract the relevant data:

- **Vertices:** Extract the vertex positions, normals, texture coordinates, and any other vertex attributes.
- **Indices:** Extract the indices that define how the vertices are connected to form triangles.
- **Materials:** Extract material information, such as diffuse color, specular color, and texture filenames.

4. Creating DirectX Resources

- **Vertex Buffer:** Create a vertex buffer and populate it with the extracted vertex data.
- **Index Buffer:** Create an index buffer and populate it with the extracted index data.
- **Textures:** Load the textures referenced by the materials and create texture resources in DirectX.

5. Rendering the 3D Model

- **Bind Resources:** Bind the vertex buffer, index buffer, and textures to the rendering pipeline.
- **Set Pipeline State:** Configure the rendering pipeline, including shaders, input layout, and other states.
- **Draw Call:** Issue a draw call to render the model using the appropriate primitive topology (usually a triangle list).

Example (Simplified):

```cpp
C++

// Load the 3D model using Assimp

Assimp::Importer importer;

const aiScene* scene = importer.ReadFile("model.obj",
aiProcess_Triangulate | aiProcess_FlipUVs);


// Extract vertex and index data
// ...


// Create vertex and index buffers
// ...


// Load textures
// ...


// Render the model

commandList->IASetPrimitiveTopology(D3D_PRIMITI
VE_TOPOLOGY_TRIANGLELIST);
```

```
commandList->IASetVertexBuffers(0,                    1,
&vertexBufferView);

commandList->IASetIndexBuffer(&indexBufferView);

commandList->DrawIndexedInstanced(numIndices, 1, 0,
0, 0);
```

Moving Forward:

By introducing 3D models into your DirectX applications, you can create rich and engaging 3D scenes. In the following chapters, we'll explore more advanced techniques for working with meshes, including mesh optimization, animation, and level of detail.

Chapter 6: Textures and Materials

Texture Mapping Fundamentals

Texture mapping is a core technique in computer graphics that brings 3D models to life by adding surface details, color, and realism. It involves wrapping 2D images (textures) around 3D objects, much like applying decorative paper onto a plain box. This process enhances visual fidelity and creates a more immersive experience.

1. The Essence of Texture Mapping

Imagine a simple 3D cube. Without textures, it appears bland and unrealistic. Texture mapping allows you to apply images, patterns, or even procedural textures to its surfaces, giving it the appearance of wood, metal, stone, or any other material.

Key Components:

- **3D Model:** The object you want to apply texture to, typically represented by a mesh of triangles.
- **Texture Image:** A 2D image that contains the color and detail you want to map onto the model's surface.
- **Texture Coordinates:** Coordinates that map each vertex of the 3D model to a corresponding

point on the texture image. These coordinates are usually in the range of [0, 1], with (0, 0) representing the top-left corner of the texture and (1, 1) representing the bottom-right corner.

2. UV Mapping

UV mapping is the process of assigning texture coordinates to the vertices of a 3D model. The "U" and "V" axes correspond to the horizontal and vertical axes of the texture image.

Creating UV Maps:

- **3D Modeling Software:** Most 3D modeling software (Blender, 3ds Max, Maya) provides tools for creating UV maps. You essentially "unwrap" the 3D model's surface into a 2D plane and then arrange the resulting UV islands (flattened faces) within the texture space.
- **Seams:** Seams are unavoidable cuts in the UV map where the 3D surface is unwrapped. These seams should be placed strategically in less visible areas to minimize visual artifacts.

3. Texture Sampling

Texture sampling is the process of retrieving color information from the texture image based on the texture coordinates provided by the vertex shader.

- **Interpolation:** The rasterizer interpolates texture coordinates across the surface of each triangle, determining the texture coordinates for each pixel (fragment).
- **Sampling:** The pixel shader uses these interpolated texture coordinates to sample the texture image and retrieve the corresponding color.
- **Filtering:** Texture filtering techniques (e.g., bilinear filtering, trilinear filtering) are used to smooth out the sampled colors and avoid pixelation.

4. Types of Textures

- **Diffuse Map:** Defines the base color of the surface.
- **Normal Map:** Adds surface details by perturbing the surface normals, creating the illusion of bumps and grooves.
- **Specular Map:** Controls the shininess and reflectivity of the surface.
- **Roughness Map:** Defines how rough or smooth the surface is, affecting how light scatters.
- **Ambient Occlusion Map:** Adds subtle shadows to crevices and contact points, enhancing realism.
- **Displacement Map:** Actually displaces the vertices of the mesh, creating true geometric details.

5. Applying Textures in DirectX

- **Create Texture Resources:** Load texture images from files and create texture resources in DirectX.
- **Create Shader Resource Views (SRVs):** Create SRVs to allow shaders to access the texture data.
- **Bind Textures:** Bind the textures to the rendering pipeline.
- **Sample in Shaders:** Use the texture.Sample function in your pixel shader to sample the texture based on the interpolated texture coordinates.

Example (HLSL Pixel Shader):

High-level shader language

```
Texture2D texture0 : register(t0);

SamplerState sampler0 : register(s0);


float4 main(VS_OUTPUT input) : SV_TARGET

{

        float4 color = texture0.Sample(sampler0, input.texcoord);

    return color;
```

}

Moving Forward:

Texture mapping is a powerful tool for adding detail and realism to your 3D scenes. In the following sections, we'll explore how to load and use textures in DirectX, implement different types of texture maps, and create more complex material properties.

Loading and Using Textures in DirectX

Now that you understand the fundamentals of texture mapping, let's dive into the practical aspects of loading and utilizing textures in your DirectX 12 applications. This involves loading image files, creating texture resources, and integrating them into your rendering pipeline.

1. Loading Texture Images

DirectX doesn't provide built-in functions for loading various image formats like PNG, JPG, or BMP. You'll need to use a third-party library or write your own image loading code.

Recommended Libraries:

- **DirectXTex:** Microsoft's DirectXTex library provides a robust set of functions for loading, saving, and manipulating images in various formats. It supports common formats like DDS, BMP, JPG, PNG, TIFF, and more.
- **WIC (Windows Imaging Component):** WIC is a built-in Windows component that supports a wide range of image formats. You can use WIC to load images and then transfer the image data to DirectX textures.
- **stb_image:** A popular, lightweight, single-header library for loading images in various formats.

Example (Loading a DDS texture with DirectXTex):

C++

```
#include <DirectXTex.h>



// ...



TexMetadata metadata;

ScratchImage image;
```

```cpp
HRESULT hr = LoadFromDDSFile(L"texture.dds",
DDS_FLAGS_NONE, &metadata, image);

if (FAILED(hr))

{

    // Handle error

}


const Image* img = image.GetImage(0, 0, 0); // Get the
first image from the scratch image


// ... (Create texture resource with img->pixels data) ...
```

2. Creating Texture Resources

Once you have the image data in memory, you need to create a texture resource in DirectX 12.

- ID3D12Device::CreateCommittedResource: Use this function to allocate memory on the GPU and create a texture resource.
- D3D12_RESOURCE_DESC: Define a D3D12_RESOURCE_DESC structure to

describe the texture's properties, such as width, height, format, mip levels, and dimension (2D, 3D, cubemap).

- **Resource States:** Specify the initial state of the texture resource (e.g., D3D12_RESOURCE_STATE_COPY_DEST if you'll be copying data to it).

Example:

C++

```
// Create a 2D texture resource

ID3D12Resource* texture;

device->CreateCommittedResource(


&CD3DX12_HEAP_PROPERTIES(D3D12_HEAP_TYPE_DEFAULT),

    D3D12_HEAP_FLAG_NONE,


&CD3DX12_RESOURCE_DESC::Tex2D(DXGI_FORMAT_R8G8B8A8_UNORM, width, height, 1, 1), // Texture description

    D3D12_RESOURCE_STATE_COPY_DEST,

    nullptr,
```

IID_PPV_ARGS(&texture));

3. Copying Texture Data

If you loaded the image data into CPU memory, you need to copy it to the GPU memory of the texture resource.

- **Upload Heap:** Create an upload heap to temporarily store the image data on the GPU.
- UpdateSubresources: Use the UpdateSubresources function to copy the image data from the upload heap to the texture resource.
- **Resource Barrier:** Transition the texture resource to the appropriate state (e.g., D3D12_RESOURCE_STATE_PIXEL_SHADER _RESOURCE) after copying the data.

4. Creating Shader Resource Views (SRVs)

To allow shaders to access the texture data, you need to create a Shader Resource View (SRV).

- D3D12_SHADER_RESOURCE_VIEW_DESC: Define a D3D12_SHADER_RESOURCE_VIEW_DESC structure to describe the SRV.

- **ID3D12Device::CreateShaderResourceView**: Use this function to create the SRV, associating it with the texture resource.

Example:

C++

```cpp
D3D12_SHADER_RESOURCE_VIEW_DESC srvDesc = {};
srvDesc.Shader4ComponentMapping = D3D12_DEFAULT_SHADER_4_COMPONENT_MAPPING;
srvDesc.Format = DXGI_FORMAT_R8G8B8A8_UNORM;
srvDesc.ViewDimension = D3D12_SRV_DIMENSION_TEXTURE2D;
srvDesc.Texture2D.MipLevels = 1;


device->CreateShaderResourceView(texture.Get(), &srvDesc, srvHeap->GetCPUDescriptorHandleForHeapStart());
```

5. Binding Textures in Shaders

- **Descriptor Tables:** Organize SRVs into descriptor tables.
- **Root Signature:** Define a root signature that includes the descriptor table.
- **Set Graphics Root Descriptor Table:** Bind the descriptor table to the rendering pipeline in your command list.
- **Sample in Shaders:** In your HLSL pixel shader, use the texture.Sample function to sample the texture based on the interpolated texture coordinates.

Example (HLSL Pixel Shader):

High-level shader language

```
Texture2D texture0 : register(t0);

SamplerState sampler0 : register(s0);


float4 main(VS_OUTPUT input) : SV_TARGET
{
        float4 color = texture0.Sample(sampler0, input.texcoord);

    return color;

}
```

Moving Forward:

With the ability to load and use textures in DirectX 12, you can significantly enhance the visual quality of your 3D scenes. In the next section, we'll explore how to use different types of texture maps to create more complex and realistic materials.

Material Properties (Diffuse, Specular, Normal)

In computer graphics, materials define how surfaces interact with light. They determine the visual appearance of objects, influencing their color, shininess, and overall realism. Let's explore three essential material properties: diffuse, specular, and normal.

1. Diffuse Reflection

Diffuse reflection is the most common type of light reflection. It occurs when light strikes a rough surface and scatters in various directions. This scattered light is what gives objects their basic color.

- **Diffuse Color:** The diffuse color of a material determines how much of the incoming light is reflected and in what color. A bright red diffuse color means the surface reflects mostly red light, while a dark gray diffuse color reflects less light overall.

- **Diffuse Map:** In texture mapping, a diffuse map (or albedo map) is an image that defines the diffuse color at each point on the surface. This allows for variations in color and patterns across the object.

2. Specular Reflection

Specular reflection is the mirror-like reflection of light from a smooth surface. It creates highlights that make objects appear shiny or glossy.

- **Specular Color:** The specular color of a material determines the color of the specular highlights. It's often white or a lighter version of the diffuse color.
- **Shininess:** Shininess (or specular exponent) controls how concentrated or spread out the specular highlights are. A higher shininess value produces smaller, sharper highlights, while a lower value creates broader, softer highlights.
- **Specular Map:** A specular map is an image that can vary the shininess across the surface, creating areas that are more or less reflective.

3. Normal Mapping

Normal mapping is a technique that adds surface details without increasing the geometric complexity of the model. It uses a normal map, which is an image that stores surface normals.

- **Surface Normals:** Surface normals are vectors that are perpendicular to the surface at each point. They determine how light interacts with the surface.
- **Normal Map:** A normal map perturbs the surface normals, creating the illusion of bumps, grooves, and other small-scale details. This adds realism without the performance cost of adding more polygons to the model.

Implementing Material Properties in DirectX

- **Material Structures:** Define structures in your code to store material properties (diffuse color, specular color, shininess).
- **Constant Buffers:** Pass material properties to your shaders using constant buffers.
- **HLSL Shaders:** In your HLSL shaders, access the material properties from the constant buffers and use them in your lighting calculations.

Example (HLSL Pixel Shader):

High-level shader language

```
cbuffer MaterialConstants : register(b0)

{

    float4 diffuseColor;

    float3 specularColor;

    float shininess;

};


// ...


float4 main(VS_OUTPUT input) : SV_TARGET

{

        // ... lighting calculations using diffuseColor,
specularColor, and shininess ...

}
```

Moving Forward:

Understanding material properties is crucial for creating realistic and visually appealing 3D objects. In the next section, we'll explore how to implement basic lighting in your DirectX applications, combining light sources with material properties to create compelling scenes.

Implementing Basic Lighting

Lighting is a crucial aspect of 3D graphics, as it breathes life into scenes and makes objects appear more realistic and three-dimensional. By simulating how light interacts with surfaces, you can create depth, highlight details, and evoke mood. Let's explore how to implement basic lighting in your DirectX applications.

1. Light Sources

In real-time graphics, we typically simulate different types of light sources:

- **Directional Light:** Simulates a light source that is infinitely far away, like the sun. It has a direction but no specific position.
- **Point Light:** Simulates a light source that emits light in all directions from a specific point, like a light bulb.
- **Spot Light:** Simulates a light source that emits a cone of light in a specific direction, like a flashlight.

Light Properties:

Each light source has properties that affect how it illuminates the scene:

- **Color:** The color of the light emitted.
- **Intensity:** The brightness of the light.
- **Direction (for directional lights):** The direction from which the light rays are coming.
- **Position (for point and spot lights):** The location of the light source in 3D space.
- **Range (for point and spot lights):** The distance over which the light's intensity diminishes.
- **Cone Angle (for spot lights):** The angle of the cone of light emitted.

2. Lighting Models

Lighting models define how light interacts with surfaces. Some common lighting models include:

- **Ambient Lighting:** Simulates the overall ambient light present in the scene. It illuminates all surfaces equally, regardless of their orientation to the light source.
- **Diffuse Lighting:** Simulates the scattering of light from rough surfaces. It depends on the angle between the surface normal and the light direction.
- **Specular Lighting:** Simulates the mirror-like reflection of light from smooth surfaces. It

creates highlights that depend on the viewer's position and the light direction.

3. Implementing Lighting in DirectX

- **Light Structures:** Define structures in your code to represent light sources and their properties.
- **Constant Buffers:** Pass light data to your shaders using constant buffers.
- **HLSL Shaders:** In your HLSL pixel shader, implement the lighting calculations using the light data and material properties.

Example (HLSL Pixel Shader with Diffuse Lighting):

High-level shader language

```
cbuffer LightConstants : register(b1)

{

    float4 lightColor;

    float3 lightDirection;

};


cbuffer MaterialConstants : register(b0)

{
```

```
    float4 diffuseColor;

    // ... other material properties ...

};


float4 main(VS_OUTPUT input) : SV_TARGET

{

    float3 normal = normalize(input.normal);

        float3 lightDir = normalize(-lightDirection); //
Direction towards the light


        float diffuseIntensity = max(dot(normal, lightDir),
0.0f); // Calculate diffuse intensity

        float4 diffuse = diffuseColor * lightColor *
diffuseIntensity;


    return diffuse;

}
```

4. Combining Lighting Models

You can combine multiple lighting models (ambient, diffuse, specular) to create more realistic lighting effects.

Example (HLSL Pixel Shader with Ambient, Diffuse, and Specular):

High-level shader language

```
// ... (Light and material constant buffers) ...


float4 main(VS_OUTPUT input) : SV_TARGET
{
    // ... (Calculate diffuse and specular lighting) ...

    float4 ambient = ambientColor * diffuseColor;
    float4 finalColor = ambient + diffuse + specular;


    return finalColor;
}
```

Moving Forward:

Implementing basic lighting brings your 3D scenes to life. In the next chapter, we'll delve deeper into lighting and shading techniques, exploring different types of light sources, more advanced lighting models, and techniques for creating realistic shadows.

Chapter 7: Transformations and Camera Control

World, View, and Projection Matrices

In 3D graphics, transforming objects from their original local space to the screen involves a series of coordinate transformations. This process is typically handled by three essential matrices: the world matrix, the view matrix, and the projection matrix. These matrices work together to position, orient, and project objects onto the 2D screen, creating the illusion of a 3D world.

1. World Matrix: Placing Objects in the World

The world matrix defines an object's position, orientation, and scale within the world coordinate system. It transforms the object's vertices from its local coordinate space (where the object is defined) to the global world space.

- **Transformations:** The world matrix can incorporate any combination of transformations, including:
  - **Translation:** Moving the object to a specific location in the world.
  - **Rotation:** Rotating the object around one or more axes.

- o **Scaling:** Resizing the object uniformly or along specific axes.
- **Uniqueness:** Each object in the scene has its own unique world matrix, allowing for independent positioning and manipulation.

2. View Matrix: Setting the Camera's Perspective

The view matrix defines the position and orientation of the camera in the world. It effectively transforms the entire scene from world space to camera space (also known as view space), where the camera is located at the origin and looking down the negative Z-axis.

- **Inverse Transformation:** The view matrix is essentially the inverse of the camera's world matrix. Instead of moving the camera, it moves the entire world in the opposite direction, creating the illusion of camera movement.
- **LookAt Function:** A common way to create a view matrix is using a "LookAt" function, which takes the camera's position, target point, and up vector as input.

3. Projection Matrix: Projecting onto the Screen

The projection matrix is responsible for projecting the 3D scene onto the 2D screen. It defines the viewing frustum, which is the region of space that is visible to the camera.

- **Perspective Projection:** Creates the illusion of depth by making objects further away appear smaller. This is the most common projection used in games and 3D applications.
- **Orthographic Projection:** Maintains parallel lines and preserves the relative sizes of objects, regardless of their distance from the camera. Often used for 2D games or technical drawings.
- **Parameters:** The projection matrix is defined by parameters such as:
  - **Field of View:** The vertical angle of the viewing frustum (for perspective projection).
  - **Aspect Ratio:** The ratio of the screen width to height.
  - **Near Plane:** The distance to the nearest visible object.
  - **Far Plane:** The distance to the farthest visible object.

4. Combining Matrices

To transform a vertex from its local space to screen space, you multiply it by the world, view, and projection matrices in that order:

transformedVertex = vertex * worldMatrix * viewMatrix * projectionMatrix;

This combined transformation efficiently positions the vertex in the world, aligns it with the camera's view, and projects it onto the screen.

5. Implementing in DirectX

- **Matrix Data Types:** DirectX provides data types like XMMATRIX to represent matrices.
- **Matrix Functions:** DirectXMath library provides functions for creating and manipulating matrices (e.g., XMMatrixTranslation, XMMatrixRotation, XMMatrixPerspectiveFovLH).
- **HLSL Shaders:** You typically pass the world, view, and projection matrices to your vertex shader as constant buffers. The vertex shader then performs the matrix multiplications to transform the vertex position.

Example (HLSL Vertex Shader):

High-level shader language

```
cbuffer          WorldViewProjectionConstantBuffer          :
register(b0)
```

```
{
    matrix worldMatrix;

    matrix viewMatrix;

    matrix projectionMatrix;
};


VS_OUTPUT main(VS_INPUT input)
{
    VS_OUTPUT output;

    float4 pos = float4(input.position, 1.0f);

    output.position = mul(pos, worldMatrix);

    output.position = mul(output.position, viewMatrix);

                output.position   =   mul(output.position,
    projectionMatrix);

    return output;
}
```

Moving Forward:

Understanding world, view, and projection matrices is fundamental to controlling the camera and positioning objects in your 3D scenes. In the next section, we'll explore how to implement camera movement and control, allowing users to navigate and interact with your 3D world.

Implementing a Camera Class

A well-structured camera class is essential for navigating and controlling the viewpoint in your 3D applications. It encapsulates the camera's properties, such as position, orientation, and projection settings, and provides methods for manipulating these properties to achieve various camera movements and effects.

1. Camera Properties

A typical camera class might include the following properties:

- **Position:** A 3D vector representing the camera's location in world space.
- **Target:** A 3D vector representing the point the camera is looking at.
- **Up Vector:** A 3D vector representing the "up" direction for the camera, usually (0, 1, 0).
- **Field of View:** The vertical angle of the camera's viewing frustum (for perspective projection).

- **Aspect Ratio:** The ratio of the screen width to height.
- **Near Plane:** The distance to the nearest visible object.
- **Far Plane:** The distance to the farthest visible object.
- **View Matrix:** A 4x4 matrix that transforms world coordinates to camera coordinates.
- **Projection Matrix:** A 4x4 matrix that projects 3D coordinates onto the 2D screen.

2. Camera Methods

The camera class should provide methods for:

- **Initialization:** Setting initial camera properties.
- **Updating View Matrix:** Recalculating the view matrix based on the camera's position, target, and up vector.
- **Updating Projection Matrix:** Recalculating the projection matrix based on the field of view, aspect ratio, near plane, and far plane.
- **Movement:** Moving the camera in various directions (forward, backward, left, right, up, down).
- **Rotation:** Rotating the camera around different axes (yaw, pitch, roll).
- **Zooming:** Adjusting the field of view to zoom in or out.

- **Getting Matrices:** Retrieving the view and projection matrices for use in shaders.

3. Example Camera Class (Simplified)

C++

```cpp
class Camera
{
public:
    Camera() :
        m_position(0.0f, 0.0f, -5.0f),
        m_target(0.0f, 0.0f, 0.0f),
        m_up(0.0f, 1.0f, 0.0f),
        m_fov(XM_PIDIV4), // 45 degrees
        m_aspectRatio(16.0f / 9.0f),
        m_nearPlane(0.1f),
        m_farPlane(100.0f)
    {
        UpdateViewMatrix();
        UpdateProjectionMatrix();
```

```cpp
    }


    void UpdateViewMatrix()
    {
        m_viewMatrix = XMMatrixLookAtLH(m_position,
m_target, m_up);
    }


    void UpdateProjectionMatrix()
    {
                                    m_projectionMatrix    =
XMMatrixPerspectiveFovLH(m_fov,      m_aspectRatio,
m_nearPlane, m_farPlane);
    }


    void Move(const XMVECTOR& direction)
    {
        m_position += direction;
        m_target += direction;
```

```cpp
        UpdateViewMatrix();
    }


    void Rotate(float yaw, float pitch, float roll)
    {
        // ... (Implement rotation logic) ...
        UpdateViewMatrix();
    }


    // ... (Other methods for zooming, getting matrices,
etc.) ...


private:
    XMVECTOR m_position;
    XMVECTOR m_target;
    XMVECTOR m_up;
    float m_fov;
    float m_aspectRatio;
```

```
float m_nearPlane;

float m_farPlane;

XMMATRIX m_viewMatrix;

XMMATRIX m_projectionMatrix;
```
};

4. Integrating with Input

To control the camera with user input, you need to:

- **Handle Input Events:** Capture keyboard and mouse input events.
- **Update Camera Properties:** Translate input events into camera movements and rotations.
- **Update Matrices:** Recalculate the view matrix after each camera movement or rotation.

Example (Handling keyboard input):

C++

```
if (GetAsyncKeyState('W') & 0x8000)

    camera.Move(XMVectorSet(0.0f, 0.0f, 0.1f, 0.0f)); //
Move forward

if (GetAsyncKeyState('S') & 0x8000)
```

```
camera.Move(XMVectorSet(0.0f, 0.0f, -0.1f, 0.0f)); //
Move backward

// ... (Handle other movement and rotation keys) ...
```

Moving Forward:

A well-implemented camera class provides a flexible and intuitive way to control the viewpoint in your 3D applications. In the next section, we'll explore different camera movement and control techniques, such as first-person, third-person, and orbit cameras.

Camera Movement and Control

Camera movement and control are crucial for creating interactive and immersive 3D experiences. They allow users to explore the virtual world, examine objects from different angles, and engage with the scene. Let's explore common camera control techniques and how to implement them in your DirectX applications.

1. First-Person Camera

The first-person camera provides a subjective view, simulating the perspective of a character within the 3D world.

- **Movement:** Movement is typically constrained to the horizontal plane (forward, backward, left, right), with the camera's "up" vector always aligned with the world's up direction.
- **Rotation:** Rotation is controlled by mouse movements, allowing the user to look around (yaw and pitch).
- **Implementation:**
  - **Input Handling:** Capture mouse movements and translate them into yaw and pitch rotations.
  - **Rotation:** Rotate the camera's view direction based on yaw and pitch.
  - **Movement:** Move the camera's position based on keyboard input (W, A, S, D) and the current view direction.

2. Third-Person Camera

The third-person camera provides an external view, following a character or object from behind and above.

- **Target:** The camera maintains a fixed offset from a target object.
- **Orbiting:** The camera can often orbit around the target, allowing the user to view the target from different angles.
- **Implementation:**

- **Target Tracking:** Update the camera's position based on the target's position and the desired offset.
- **Orbiting:** Implement rotation logic to orbit the camera around the target based on mouse input.
- **Collision Detection:** Consider implementing collision detection to prevent the camera from clipping through objects.

3. Orbit Camera

The orbit camera revolves around a fixed point in space, allowing the user to view the scene from different angles.

- **Focus Point:** The camera maintains a fixed distance from a focus point.
- **Rotation:** The camera can rotate around the focus point (yaw, pitch).
- **Zooming:** The camera can move closer or farther from the focus point.
- **Implementation:**
  - **Spherical Coordinates:** Represent the camera's position using spherical coordinates (radius, azimuth, inclination).
  - **Rotation:** Update the azimuth and inclination angles based on mouse input.

- Zooming: Adjust the radius based on mouse wheel input or other controls.

4. Free Camera

The free camera allows unrestricted movement and rotation in all directions.

- **Movement:** The camera can move freely in 3D space.
- **Rotation:** The camera can rotate freely around all axes.
- **Implementation:**
    - **Combine Movements:** Combine keyboard input (W, A, S, D, Q, E) to move the camera in different directions.
    - **Combine Rotations:** Combine mouse input to rotate the camera around different axes.

5. Smoothing Camera Movement

To create smoother camera movements, you can use techniques like:

- **Interpolation:** Interpolate the camera's position and orientation over time.
- **Damping:** Apply damping to the camera's movement and rotation to reduce abrupt changes.

6. Considerations

- **Frame Rate Independence:** Ensure that camera movement is independent of the frame rate to maintain consistent speed across different systems.
- **Input Sensitivity:** Allow users to adjust the sensitivity of mouse and keyboard input for personalized control.
- **Collision Avoidance:** Implement collision detection and avoidance to prevent the camera from getting stuck in objects or going through walls.

Moving Forward:

Implementing various camera movement and control techniques enhances the interactivity and immersion of your 3D applications. As you experiment with different camera types and controls, you'll discover new ways to engage users and create compelling 3D experiences.

Perspective and Orthographic Projections

Projection is the final step in the transformation pipeline, responsible for converting the 3D scene into a 2D image that can be displayed on the screen. Two primary projection methods are used in computer graphics: perspective projection and orthographic projection. Each offers a distinct way of representing the 3D world, with different visual characteristics and applications.

1. Perspective Projection

Perspective projection mimics how we perceive the real world. Objects further away appear smaller, and parallel lines converge towards a vanishing point, creating a sense of depth and realism.

- **Viewing Frustum:** The viewing frustum in perspective projection is shaped like a truncated pyramid. It defines the region of space that is visible to the camera.
- **Depth Perception:** The key characteristic of perspective projection is that it preserves depth information. Objects closer to the camera appear larger on the screen, while objects further away appear smaller, creating a natural sense of distance.
- **Applications:** Perspective projection is widely used in games, simulations, and 3D visualizations where realism and depth perception are crucial.

2. Orthographic Projection

Orthographic projection, in contrast, maintains parallel lines and preserves the relative sizes of objects, regardless of their distance from the camera. It's like viewing the scene from an infinite distance.

- **Viewing Volume:** The viewing volume in orthographic projection is shaped like a box.

- **No Depth Scaling:** Objects maintain their true size and shape, regardless of their distance from the camera. This eliminates perspective foreshortening.
- **Applications:** Orthographic projection is commonly used in:
  - **2D Games:** Where maintaining the true size of sprites and objects is important.
  - **Architectural and Engineering Drawings:** Where accurate measurements and proportions are crucial.
  - **Technical Illustrations:** Where clarity and precise representation of objects are needed.

Implementing Projections in DirectX

- **Projection Matrix:** Both perspective and orthographic projections are represented by a 4x4 projection matrix.
- **DirectXMath Functions:** The DirectXMath library provides functions for creating projection matrices:
  - XMMatrixPerspectiveFovLH: Creates a perspective projection matrix.
  - XMMatrixOrthographicLH: Creates an orthographic projection matrix.
- **Parameters:** You provide parameters to these functions to define the projection:

- Perspective: Field of view, aspect ratio, near plane, far plane.
- Orthographic: View width, view height, near plane, far plane.

Example (Creating a perspective projection matrix):

C++

```
XMMATRIX                projectionMatrix            =
XMMatrixPerspectiveFovLH(

    XM_PIDIV4, // Field of view (45 degrees)

    aspectRatio, // Aspect ratio

    0.1f, // Near plane

    100.0f // Far plane
);
```

Choosing the Right Projection

The choice between perspective and orthographic projection depends on the specific needs of your application. Consider the following factors:

- **Realism:** Perspective projection provides a more realistic view, while orthographic projection offers a more technical or schematic representation.

- **Depth Perception:** If depth perception is crucial, use perspective projection.
- **Object Size:** If maintaining the true size of objects is important, use orthographic projection.

Moving Forward:

Understanding perspective and orthographic projections is essential for controlling how your 3D scenes are presented on the screen. As you experiment with different projection settings and camera controls, you'll gain a deeper understanding of how to create various visual effects and immersive 3D experiences.

Chapter 8: Lighting and Shading

Lighting plays a pivotal role in shaping the visual perception of 3D scenes. It adds depth, reveals surface details, and creates a sense of realism. In this section, we'll explore three fundamental lighting components: ambient, diffuse, and specular lighting. These components, when combined, simulate the way light interacts with surfaces, producing a wide range of lighting effects.

1. Ambient Lighting

Ambient lighting represents the overall background illumination present in a scene. It's a subtle, directionless light that affects all surfaces equally, regardless of their orientation to any specific light source.

- **Simulating Indirect Light:** Ambient light approximates the effect of light bouncing off multiple surfaces in the environment, creating a soft, ambient glow.
- **Uniform Illumination:** It ensures that even surfaces not directly lit by a light source are not completely dark.

- **Implementation:** Ambient lighting is usually implemented by multiplying the ambient light color with the surface's diffuse color.

Example (HLSL Pixel Shader):

High-level shader language

float4 ambient = ambientColor * material.diffuseColor;

2. Diffuse Lighting

Diffuse lighting simulates the scattering of light from rough surfaces. It's the primary component that gives objects their base color and defines their overall illumination.

- **Direction Dependent:** The intensity of diffuse light depends on the angle between the surface normal and the direction of the light source.
- **Lambert's Cosine Law:** Diffuse reflection follows Lambert's cosine law, which states that the intensity of reflected light is proportional to the cosine of the angle between the light direction and the surface normal.
- **Implementation:** Diffuse lighting is calculated using the dot product of the surface normal and the light direction.

Example (HLSL Pixel Shader):

High-level shader language

```
float3 lightDir = normalize(light.position - input.worldPos); // Direction towards the light

float3 normal = normalize(input.normal);

float diffuseIntensity = max(dot(normal, lightDir), 0.0f); // Calculate diffuse intensity

float4 diffuse = material.diffuseColor * light.color * diffuseIntensity;
```

3. Specular Lighting

Specular lighting simulates the bright highlights that appear on shiny surfaces when light reflects directly towards the viewer. It adds a sense of glossiness and reflectivity to objects.

- **View Dependent:** The intensity of specular light depends on the angle between the reflected light vector and the viewer's direction.
- **Phong Reflection Model:** A common model for specular lighting is the Phong reflection model, which uses the dot product of the reflected light

vector and the view direction raised to a power (shininess exponent).

- **Implementation:** Specular lighting is calculated using the dot product of the reflected light vector and the view direction, along with the material's specular color and shininess.

Example (HLSL Pixel Shader):

High-level shader language

```
float3 viewDir = normalize(cameraPosition - input.worldPos); // Direction towards the viewer

float3 reflectDir = reflect(-lightDir, normal); // Calculate reflected light direction

float specularIntensity = pow(max(dot(viewDir, reflectDir), 0.0f), material.shininess);

float4 specular = material.specularColor * light.color * specularIntensity;
```

Combining Lighting Components

To achieve realistic lighting, you typically combine ambient, diffuse, and specular lighting components:

High-level shader language

```
float4 finalColor = ambient + diffuse + specular;
```

Considerations

- **Attenuation:** For point and spot lights, you should consider attenuation, which is the decrease in light intensity over distance.
- **Multiple Lights:** You can extend the lighting calculations to handle multiple light sources in the scene.
- **Optimization:** There are various techniques for optimizing lighting calculations, such as precomputing lighting data or using lightmaps.

Moving Forward:

Understanding ambient, diffuse, and specular lighting provides the foundation for creating realistic and visually engaging scenes. In the next section, we'll delve deeper into lighting techniques, exploring different types of light sources, shadowing, and more advanced shading models.

Light Sources (Directional, Point, Spot)

In 3D graphics, simulating various types of light sources is essential for achieving realistic and visually compelling scenes. Each light source type has unique characteristics and applications, influencing how objects are illuminated and how shadows are cast. Let's explore three common light source types: directional, point, and spot.

1. Directional Light

A directional light simulates a light source that is infinitely far away, such as the sun. It has a direction but no specific position.

- **Parallel Rays:** Light rays from a directional light are considered parallel, illuminating all objects in the scene with the same intensity regardless of their distance from the light source.
- **Uniform Lighting:** This creates a consistent lighting effect across the scene, ideal for simulating sunlight or other distant light sources.
- **Properties:**
  - **Direction:** A 3D vector representing the direction from which the light rays are coming.
  - **Color:** The color of the emitted light.
  - **Intensity:** The brightness of the light.

2. Point Light

A point light simulates a light source that emits light in all directions from a specific point, like a light bulb.

- **Radial Attenuation:** The intensity of a point light decreases as the distance from the light source increases. This attenuation can be controlled using various falloff functions (linear, quadratic, etc.).
- **Omnidirectional Illumination:** A point light illuminates objects in all directions around its position.
- **Properties:**
  - **Position:** A 3D vector representing the location of the light source in world space.
  - **Color:** The color of the emitted light.
  - **Intensity:** The brightness of the light.
  - **Range:** The distance over which the light's intensity diminishes.

3. Spot Light

A spot light simulates a light source that emits a cone of light in a specific direction, like a flashlight or a spotlight in a theater.

- **Directional and Attenuated:** It combines the directional aspect of a directional light with the attenuation of a point light.
- **Cone Shape:** The light's intensity is strongest along the central axis of the cone and decreases towards the edges.

- **Properties:**
  - **Position:** A 3D vector representing the location of the light source in world space.
  - **Direction:** A 3D vector representing the direction of the cone's central axis.
  - **Color:** The color of the emitted light.
  - **Intensity:** The brightness of the light.
  - **Range:** The distance over which the light's intensity diminishes.
  - **Cone Angle:** The angle of the cone of light emitted.
  - **Falloff:** The rate at which the light intensity decreases from the center to the edges of the cone.

Implementing Light Sources in DirectX

- **Light Structures:** Define structures in your code to represent each light source type and its properties.
- **Constant Buffers:** Pass light data to your shaders using constant buffers.
- **HLSL Shaders:** In your HLSL shaders, access the light data from the constant buffers and use it in your lighting calculations.

Example (HLSL Constant Buffer for a Point Light):

High-level shader language

```
cbuffer PointLight : register(b1)

{

    float4 position;

    float4 color;

    float range;

};
```

Choosing the Right Light Source

The choice of light source depends on the desired effect and the scene's requirements.

- **Sunlight:** Use a directional light to simulate sunlight.
- **Light Bulbs:** Use point lights to simulate light bulbs or other omnidirectional light sources.
- **Flashlights:** Use spot lights to simulate flashlights, headlights, or other focused light sources.

Moving Forward:

Understanding and implementing different light source types is crucial for creating diverse and realistic lighting scenarios. In the next section, we'll explore how to implement lighting calculations in shaders, combining light sources with material properties to achieve various lighting effects.

Implementing Lighting in Shaders

Shaders provide the flexibility and power to implement various lighting models and calculations, allowing you to achieve a wide range of lighting effects in your 3D scenes. Let's explore how to implement lighting calculations within your HLSL shaders, combining light source properties with material properties to create realistic illumination.

1. Passing Data to Shaders

Before you can perform lighting calculations in your shaders, you need to pass the necessary data from your C++ code:

- **Light Data:** Create structures in your C++ code to represent light sources and their properties (position, direction, color, intensity, etc.).
- **Material Data:** Define structures to hold material properties (diffuse color, specular color, shininess, etc.).
- **Constant Buffers:** Use constant buffers to efficiently pass light and material data to your shaders each frame.

Example (HLSL Constant Buffers):

High-level shader language

```
cbuffer LightConstants : register(b1)
{
    float4 lightColor;
    float3 lightDirection;
    float4 lightPosition;
    // ... other light properties ...
};


cbuffer MaterialConstants : register(b0)
{
    float4 diffuseColor;
    float3 specularColor;
    float shininess;
    // ... other material properties ...
};
```

2. Vertex Shader Responsibilities

The vertex shader plays a crucial role in preparing data for lighting calculations in the pixel shader:

- **World Position:** Calculate the world position of the vertex and pass it to the pixel shader.
- **Normal Vector:** Transform the vertex normal to world space and pass it to the pixel shader.
- **View Direction:** Calculate the view direction (from the vertex to the camera) and pass it to the pixel shader (optional, can be calculated in pixel shader as well).

Example (HLSL Vertex Shader):

High-level shader language

```
VS_OUTPUT main(VS_INPUT input)
{
    VS_OUTPUT output;
        output.position = mul(float4(input.position, 1.0f), worldMatrix); // Calculate world position
    output.worldPos = output.position.xyz;
    output.position = mul(output.position, viewMatrix);
```

```
        output.position   =   mul(output.position,
projectionMatrix);

        output.normal   =   mul(input.normal,
(float3x3)worldMatrix); // Transform normal to world
space

    return output;

}
```

3. Pixel Shader Calculations

The pixel shader is where the core lighting calculations take place:

- **Access Data:** Access light and material data from the constant buffers.
- **Calculate Light Direction:** Calculate the direction from the pixel to the light source (for point and spot lights).
- **Normalize Vectors:** Normalize the normal vector and light direction for accurate calculations.
- **Ambient Lighting:** Calculate the ambient lighting component.

- **Diffuse Lighting:** Calculate the diffuse lighting component using the dot product of the normal and light direction.
- **Specular Lighting:** Calculate the specular lighting component using the Phong reflection model or other specular models.
- **Combine Components:** Combine the ambient, diffuse, and specular components to get the final pixel color.

Example (HLSL Pixel Shader):

High-level shader language

```
float4 main(VS_OUTPUT input) : SV_TARGET
{
        float3 lightDir = normalize(lightPosition.xyz - input.worldPos);

    float3 normal = normalize(input.normal);

        float3 viewDir = normalize(cameraPosition - input.worldPos);


    // Ambient
            float4 ambient = ambientColor * material.diffuseColor;
```

```
    // Diffuse
    float diffuseIntensity = max(dot(normal, lightDir),
0.0f);
    float4 diffuse = material.diffuseColor * lightColor *
diffuseIntensity;


    // Specular (Phong)
    float3 reflectDir = reflect(-lightDir, normal);
    float specularIntensity = pow(max(dot(viewDir,
reflectDir), 0.0f), material.shininess);
    float4 specular = material.specularColor * lightColor
* specularIntensity;


    float4 finalColor = ambient + diffuse + specular;
    return finalColor;
}
```

4. Optimization Considerations

- **Precomputing:** Precompute lighting information whenever possible (e.g., for static objects and lights) to reduce per-pixel calculations.
- **Lightmaps:** Use lightmaps to store precomputed lighting information as textures, reducing the need for complex lighting calculations in the shader.
- **Shader Optimizations:** Optimize your shader code to minimize redundant calculations and improve performance.

Moving Forward:

Implementing lighting in shaders is a key step towards creating realistic and visually engaging 3D scenes. As you explore different lighting models, techniques, and optimizations, you'll gain a deeper understanding of how to manipulate light and shadow to achieve various artistic and visual effects.

Basic Shading Models (Gouraud, Phong)

Shading models determine how the color of a surface is calculated, taking into account lighting, material properties, and the orientation of the surface. They play a crucial role in creating the visual appearance of objects, influencing their smoothness, shininess, and overall realism. Let's explore two fundamental shading models: Gouraud shading and Phong shading.

1. Gouraud Shading

Gouraud shading, also known as per-vertex shading, is a relatively simple and computationally efficient shading model.

- **Vertex-Based Calculation:** Lighting calculations (ambient, diffuse, specular) are performed at each vertex of the mesh.
- **Interpolation:** The resulting colors at the vertices are then interpolated across the surface of each triangle to determine the color of each pixel.
- **Advantages:**
  - **Efficiency:** Less computationally expensive than Phong shading because lighting calculations are done per vertex, not per pixel.
- **Disadvantages:**
  - **Mach Bands:** Can produce noticeable Mach bands (visual artifacts that exaggerate the contrast between adjacent polygons) along the edges of polygons.
  - **Highlight Distortion:** Specular highlights can be distorted or missed if they fall within the interior of a polygon.

2. Phong Shading

Phong shading, also known as per-pixel shading, is a more sophisticated shading model that produces smoother and more realistic results.

- **Pixel-Based Calculation:** Lighting calculations are performed at each pixel (fragment) of the rendered image.
- **Interpolation:** Instead of interpolating colors, Phong shading interpolates the vertex normals across the surface of each triangle. These interpolated normals are then used in the per-pixel lighting calculations.
- **Advantages:**
    - **Smoothness:** Produces smoother shading and more accurate specular highlights.
    - **Realism:** Creates a more realistic appearance, especially for curved surfaces.
- **Disadvantages:**
    - **Performance:** More computationally expensive than Gouraud shading because lighting calculations are done per pixel.

Implementing Shading Models in DirectX

- **Shader Code:** The shading model is implemented within your HLSL shaders.
- **Gouraud Shading:**

- o Perform lighting calculations in the vertex shader.
- o Output the resulting color from the vertex shader.
- o The pixel shader simply uses the interpolated color.
- **Phong Shading:**
  - o Pass the vertex normals from the vertex shader to the pixel shader.
  - o Perform lighting calculations in the pixel shader using the interpolated normals.

Example (HLSL Code for Phong Shading):

High-level shader language

```
// Vertex Shader

VS_OUTPUT main(VS_INPUT input)

{
    // ...

            output.normal    =    mul(input.normal,
(float3x3)worldMatrix); // Pass normal to pixel shader

    // ...

}
```

```
// Pixel Shader

float4 main(VS_OUTPUT input) : SV_TARGET

{

        float3   normal   =   normalize(input.normal);   //
Interpolated normal

   // ... (lighting calculations using normal) ...

}
```

Choosing the Right Shading Model

The choice between Gouraud shading and Phong shading depends on the balance between performance and visual quality.

- **Performance Critical:** If performance is a major concern, Gouraud shading might be a better choice.
- **Visual Quality:** If visual fidelity and smooth shading are paramount, Phong shading is preferred.
- **Modern Hardware:** Modern GPUs are generally powerful enough to handle Phong shading for most applications.

Moving Forward:

Understanding Gouraud and Phong shading provides a foundation for implementing various shading effects in your DirectX applications. As you explore more advanced shading techniques, you can create even more realistic and visually compelling 3D scenes.

Part III: Advanced Topics

Chapter 9: Performance Optimization

Profiling and Benchmarking

In the world of real-time graphics, performance is paramount. Smooth frame rates and responsive interactions are crucial for creating immersive and enjoyable experiences. Profiling and benchmarking are essential techniques for analyzing performance, identifying bottlenecks, and optimizing your DirectX applications to achieve the best possible results.

1. Profiling: Identifying Performance Hotspots

Profiling involves measuring the time spent in different parts of your application to pinpoint performance bottlenecks. It helps you understand where your application is spending most of its CPU and GPU time, allowing you to focus your optimization efforts on the most critical areas.

Profiling Tools:

- **Visual Studio Profiler:** Visual Studio comes with built-in profiling tools that can analyze CPU usage, GPU usage, and other performance metrics.

- **PIX:** PIX is a powerful graphics debugging and profiling tool from Microsoft, specifically designed for DirectX applications. It provides detailed insights into GPU performance, including shader execution time, memory access patterns, and pipeline stalls.
- **GPU Vendors' Tools:** GPU vendors like NVIDIA (Nsight Graphics) and AMD (Radeon GPU Profiler) offer their own profiling tools with specific features and insights into their respective hardware.

Profiling Techniques:

- **Instrumentation:** Adding timing code to your application to measure the execution time of specific functions or code blocks.
- **Sampling:** Periodically capturing the call stack and performance counters to get a statistical overview of where time is being spent.
- **Tracing:** Recording detailed events and timing information related to GPU activity.

2. Benchmarking: Measuring Overall Performance

Benchmarking involves running controlled tests to measure the overall performance of your application under different conditions. It helps you:

- **Establish a Baseline:** Measure the initial performance of your application before making any optimizations.
- **Evaluate Optimizations:** Measure the performance gains achieved by applying various optimization techniques.
- **Compare Performance:** Compare the performance of your application across different hardware configurations or against other applications.

Benchmarking Best Practices:

- **Controlled Environment:** Run benchmarks in a controlled environment to minimize external factors that could affect the results.
- **Representative Workloads:** Use realistic workloads that represent typical usage scenarios for your application.
- **Multiple Runs:** Run benchmarks multiple times and average the results to reduce variability.
- **Measure Relevant Metrics:** Measure frame rate, frame time, CPU usage, GPU usage, and other relevant metrics.
- **Compare Apples to Apples:** Ensure that you are comparing performance under equivalent conditions when evaluating different optimizations or hardware.

3. Analyzing Results and Optimizing

Once you have profiling and benchmarking data, you can analyze the results to identify performance bottlenecks and apply optimization techniques.

- **CPU Bottlenecks:**
    - ○ **Reduce Draw Calls:** Batch geometry to minimize the number of draw calls.
    - ○ **Optimize Algorithms:** Improve the efficiency of your game logic and algorithms.
    - ○ **Multithreading:** Utilize multithreading to parallelize tasks and utilize multiple CPU cores.
- **GPU Bottlenecks:**
    - ○ **Optimize Shaders:** Reduce complexity, minimize texture fetches, and use efficient algorithms.
    - ○ **Reduce Overdraw:** Avoid rendering pixels that will be hidden by other objects.
    - ○ **Optimize Resource Usage:** Use efficient texture formats, minimize memory bandwidth usage, and manage resource states effectively.

4. Iterative Process

Performance optimization is an iterative process. You should:

- **Profile:** Identify performance hotspots.
- **Benchmark:** Measure baseline performance.
- **Optimize:** Apply optimization techniques.
- **Benchmark Again:** Measure the performance gains.
- **Repeat:** Continue profiling, benchmarking, and optimizing until you achieve your performance goals.

Moving Forward:

Profiling and benchmarking are essential tools in your DirectX performance optimization arsenal. By understanding how to use these techniques effectively, you can identify bottlenecks, apply optimizations, and achieve smooth and responsive graphics in your applications. In the following sections, we'll explore specific optimization techniques for both CPU and GPU, helping you maximize the performance of your DirectX applications.

Draw Call Batching

Draw call batching is a crucial optimization technique that focuses on reducing the CPU overhead associated with rendering. Each draw call requires the CPU to send a set of commands to the GPU, which can be a significant bottleneck, especially when rendering scenes with many objects. By batching multiple objects into a single draw call, you can minimize this overhead and improve rendering performance.

1. The Cost of Draw Calls

Every time you issue a draw call, the CPU needs to:

- **Set Pipeline State:** Configure the rendering pipeline (shaders, input layout, etc.).
- **Set Render Targets:** Bind the render targets and depth-stencil buffer.
- **Set Vertex and Index Buffers:** Bind the vertex and index buffers for the object being drawn.
- **Set Constant Buffers:** Update and bind constant buffers for object-specific data (world matrix, material properties, etc.).
- **Submit Draw Command:** Send the draw command to the GPU, specifying the primitive topology and the number of vertices or indices to draw.

This process involves communication between the CPU and GPU, which can be relatively expensive in terms of performance.

2. Batching Techniques

- **Geometry Batching:** Combine multiple objects with the same material and rendering state into a single vertex and index buffer. This allows you to render them with a single draw call.

- **Instancing:** Render multiple instances of the same object with a single draw call, using instancing techniques. Each instance can have different transformations (position, rotation, scale) applied to it.
- **Sorting:** Sort objects by their rendering state (material, textures, shaders) to minimize state changes between draw calls.

3. Benefits of Batching

- **Reduced CPU Overhead:** Significantly reduces the number of draw calls, minimizing CPU workload and communication overhead with the GPU.
- **Improved Rendering Performance:** Allows the GPU to render more objects with less overhead, potentially increasing frame rate.
- **Reduced State Changes:** Minimizes the number of times the rendering pipeline needs to be reconfigured, improving efficiency.

4. Implementing Batching in DirectX 12

- **Geometry Batching:**
  - **Combine Meshes:** Combine the vertex and index data of multiple objects into larger buffers.

- Adjust Indices: Offset the indices in the index buffer to account for the combined vertex data.
- Single Draw Call: Render the combined geometry with a single draw call.
- **Instancing:**
  - **Instance Buffer:** Create an instance buffer to store per-instance data (e.g., world matrix).
  - DrawIndexedInstanced: Use the DrawIndexedInstanced function to render multiple instances with a single draw call.
- **Sorting:**
  - **Sort Objects:** Sort objects by their rendering state before rendering.
  - **Minimize State Changes:** Group objects with the same state together to reduce pipeline state changes.

5. Considerations

- **Batching Limits:** There are limits to how much geometry you can batch together. Excessively large buffers can negatively impact performance due to increased memory usage and cache misses.
- **Dynamic Objects:** Batching is most effective for static objects. Dynamic objects that change

frequently might require more dynamic batching strategies or individual draw calls.

Moving Forward:

Draw call batching is a fundamental optimization technique that can significantly improve the performance of your DirectX applications. By understanding how to implement various batching strategies, you can minimize CPU overhead and allow the GPU to focus on rendering, leading to smoother and more responsive graphics. In the next section, we'll explore other optimization techniques, such as resource management and shader optimization.

Resource Management

Efficient resource management is crucial for achieving optimal performance in DirectX 12 applications. Resources, such as textures, buffers, and descriptor heaps, consume valuable GPU memory and bandwidth. Careful management of these resources can significantly impact rendering performance and overall application stability. Let's explore key aspects of resource management in DirectX 12.

1. Memory Allocation

- **Committed Resources:** DirectX 12 primarily uses committed resources, where memory is allocated from the GPU heap and dedicated to a specific resource.

- **Placed Resources:** For advanced scenarios, you can use placed resources to allocate memory within a specific heap region, providing more control over memory layout.
- **Reserved Resources:** Reserved resources allow you to reserve a virtual address range without immediate memory backing, useful for dynamic allocation.

2. Resource States

- **State Tracking:** DirectX 12 requires explicit tracking of resource states. Each resource exists in a specific state (e.g., D3D12_RESOURCE_STATE_GENERIC_READ, D3D12_RESOURCE_STATE_RENDER_TARGET, D3D12_RESOURCE_STATE_PIXEL_SHADER_RESOURCE) that determines how it can be accessed by the GPU.
- **Resource Barriers:** Use resource barriers to transition resources between states. This ensures correct synchronization and prevents hazards when accessing resources from different parts of the rendering pipeline.

3. Descriptor Heaps

- **Managing Descriptors:** Descriptor heaps are blocks of memory that store descriptors, which are small data structures that describe resources to the GPU.
- **Descriptor Types:** DirectX 12 uses different types of descriptor heaps for different types of descriptors (CBV_SRV_UAV, Sampler, RTV, DSV).
- **Allocation:** Allocate descriptors from the heap and associate them with resources.
- **Descriptor Tables:** Organize descriptors into descriptor tables for efficient binding in shaders.

4. Resource Lifetime

- **Creation and Destruction:** Create resources during initialization or as needed, and release them when they are no longer required.
- **Reference Counting:** DirectX 12 uses COM (Component Object Model) for resource management. Keep track of resource references and release them properly to avoid memory leaks.

5. Uploading and Updating Resources

- **Upload Heaps:** Use upload heaps to efficiently transfer data from CPU memory to GPU memory.

- **UpdateSubresources:** Use the UpdateSubresources function to copy data to resources.
- **Dynamic Updates:** For dynamic resources that change frequently, consider using mappable buffers or other techniques to update data efficiently.

6. Optimizations

- **Reuse Resources:** Reuse resources whenever possible to avoid frequent allocation and deallocation.
- **Minimize Resource Creation:** Create resources upfront during initialization if their properties don't change frequently.
- **Efficient Texture Formats:** Choose appropriate texture formats that balance visual quality with memory usage.
- **Mipmapping:** Use mipmaps to improve texture sampling performance and reduce aliasing.
- **Memory Alignment:** Align resource memory allocations to optimize data access by the GPU.

7. Tools and Techniques

- **PIX:** Use PIX to analyze resource usage, identify memory leaks, and track resource state transitions.

- **GPU Debugging Tools:** Utilize GPU debugging tools from vendors like NVIDIA and AMD to monitor memory usage and identify performance issues.

Moving Forward:

Efficient resource management is crucial for achieving optimal performance and stability in your DirectX 12 applications. By understanding resource allocation, states, descriptor heaps, and lifetime management, you can effectively utilize GPU resources and avoid common pitfalls. In the next section, we'll explore shader optimization techniques to further enhance rendering performance.

Shader Optimization Techniques

Shaders are the heart of the rendering pipeline, responsible for transforming vertices and calculating pixel colors. Optimizing your shaders is crucial for achieving high frame rates and smooth visuals in your DirectX applications. Here are some essential shader optimization techniques to help you get the most out of your graphics hardware.

1. Reduce Complexity

- **Simplify Calculations:** Avoid unnecessary calculations and complex mathematical operations whenever possible.
- **Minimize Branching:** Reduce the use of conditional statements (if, else) and loops, as they can disrupt instruction flow and introduce branching overhead.
- **Use Built-in Functions:** Leverage HLSL's built-in functions, which are often optimized for the underlying hardware.

2. Optimize Texture Access

- **Minimize Texture Fetches:** Reduce the number of texture samples by reusing sampled values or using textures with lower resolutions when appropriate.
- **Efficient Filtering:** Choose appropriate texture filtering modes (e.g., bilinear, trilinear, anisotropic) to balance visual quality with performance.
- **Texture Atlases:** Combine multiple textures into a single texture atlas to reduce texture binding overhead.

3. Optimize Memory Access

- **Data Locality:** Organize shader data (constants, variables) to improve memory access patterns and cache utilization.

- **Avoid Dynamic Indexing:** Minimize the use of dynamic indexing into arrays, as it can lead to inefficient memory access.
- **Use Constant Buffers Effectively:** Keep frequently accessed data in constant buffers, which are optimized for fast access.

4. Utilize Shader Features

- **Early Discarding:** Use clip() or discard in the pixel shader to discard fragments early, avoiding unnecessary calculations.
- **Specialized Instructions:** Utilize specialized instructions (e.g., sincos, mad) when available, as they can be more efficient than separate instructions.
- **Derivatives:** Use derivative functions (ddx, ddy) carefully, as they can introduce overhead.

5. Compiler Optimizations

- **Optimization Levels:** Use appropriate optimization levels during shader compilation (/O1, /O2, /Ox) to allow the compiler to perform optimizations.
- **Shader Model:** Target a specific shader model that balances features with performance for your target hardware.

6. Profiling and Analysis

- **Shader Profiling:** Use profiling tools (PIX, GPU vendor tools) to identify performance bottlenecks within your shaders.
- **Analyze Shader Assembly:** Examine the generated shader assembly code to understand how your HLSL code is translated and identify potential optimizations.

7. Avoid Common Pitfalls

- **Overusing Temporary Variables:** Minimize the use of temporary variables, as they can consume registers and increase register pressure.
- **Unnecessary Precision:** Use the appropriate data types and precision (e.g., float, half) to avoid unnecessary calculations.
- **Redundant Calculations:** Avoid repeating the same calculations multiple times within a shader.

Moving Forward:

Shader optimization is an iterative process that involves analyzing performance, applying optimization techniques, and measuring the results. By understanding the principles of shader optimization and leveraging the available tools and techniques, you can significantly improve the performance of your DirectX applications and create smooth, visually stunning experiences. In the next chapter, we'll explore how to work with meshes, including loading, processing, and optimizing 3D models.

Chapter 10: Working with Meshes

Loading 3D Models (OBJ, FBX)

While creating simple geometric shapes within your DirectX application is useful for learning the basics, most real-world scenarios involve loading complex 3D models created in external modeling software. These models bring richness and detail to your scenes, representing characters, environments, and objects with intricate geometries and textures. In this section, we'll explore how to load two popular 3D model formats – OBJ and FBX – into your DirectX applications.

1. Understanding 3D Model Formats

- **OBJ (Wavefront OBJ):** A simple text-based format that stores vertex positions, normals, texture coordinates, and face definitions. It's relatively easy to parse but lacks support for complex features like animations and skeletal hierarchies.
- **FBX (Autodesk FBX):** A more versatile binary format that can store a wide range of data, including meshes, animations, skeletal structures, materials, and lighting. It's widely used in the game industry and other 3D applications.

2. Loading Libraries

DirectX doesn't provide built-in functions for loading 3D models directly from these file formats. You'll need to use a third-party library to handle the parsing and data extraction.

- **Assimp (Open Asset Import Library):** A powerful and versatile library that supports a wide variety of 3D model formats, including OBJ, FBX, glTF, and more. It handles parsing the files, loading the data, and converting it into a format suitable for use in DirectX.
- **DirectXMesh:** A Microsoft library that provides helper functions for loading and processing meshes, including loading from .sdkmesh files (a DirectX-specific format) and generating tangent frames.

3. Loading OBJ Models with Assimp

C++

```cpp
#include <assimp/Importer.hpp>

#include <assimp/scene.h>

#include <assimp/postprocess.h>


// ...
```

```cpp
// Create an Assimp importer

Assimp::Importer importer;


// Load the OBJ model with post-processing options

const aiScene* scene = importer.ReadFile("model.obj",

        aiProcess_Triangulate  |  aiProcess_FlipUVs  |
aiProcess_CalcTangentSpace);


// Check for errors

if      (!scene      ||      scene->mFlags      &
AI_SCENE_FLAGS_INCOMPLETE                      ||
!scene->mRootNode)

{

    // Handle error

}


// Process the scene data (extract vertices, indices,
materials, etc.)

ProcessNode(scene->mRootNode, scene);
```

// ...

4. Loading FBX Models with Assimp

Loading FBX models follows a similar process:

C++

// ...

```
// Load the FBX model
const aiScene* scene = importer.ReadFile("model.fbx",
        aiProcess_Triangulate | aiProcess_FlipUVs |
aiProcess_CalcTangentSpace);


// ... (Process the scene data) ...
```

5. Processing Scene Data

Once the model is loaded, you need to traverse the scene hierarchy and extract the relevant data:

- **Meshes:** Access the aiMesh objects to extract vertex positions, normals, texture coordinates, and indices.
- **Materials:** Access the aiMaterial objects to extract material properties (diffuse color, specular color, textures, etc.).
- **Nodes:** Traverse the scene graph using aiNode objects to get the transformation hierarchy of the model.

6. Creating DirectX Resources

After extracting the data, create the necessary DirectX resources:

- **Vertex Buffers:** Create vertex buffers and populate them with the extracted vertex data.
- **Index Buffers:** Create index buffers and populate them with the extracted index data.
- **Textures:** Load the textures referenced by the materials and create texture resources in DirectX.

7. Rendering the Model

- **Bind Resources:** Bind the vertex buffers, index buffers, and textures to the rendering pipeline.
- **Set Pipeline State:** Configure the rendering pipeline with the appropriate shaders and states.

- **Draw Call:** Issue a draw call to render the model using the extracted index data and the appropriate primitive topology.

8. Considerations

- **Error Handling:** Implement robust error handling to gracefully handle invalid model files or missing data.
- **Optimization:** Optimize the model data (e.g., vertex caching, index optimization) to improve rendering performance.
- **Animation:** If the model contains animation data, you'll need to implement animation processing and skeletal animation techniques.

Moving Forward:

Loading 3D models from external sources significantly expands the possibilities for creating rich and detailed 3D scenes in your DirectX applications. By utilizing libraries like Assimp and understanding the process of extracting and utilizing model data, you can bring complex characters, environments, and objects to life in your virtual worlds. In the next section, we'll explore how to work with mesh data structures and optimize them for efficient rendering.

Mesh Data Structures

3D models are typically composed of meshes, which are collections of vertices, faces, and other attributes that define the shape and structure of the object. Efficiently storing and accessing this mesh data is crucial for rendering and manipulating 3D models in your DirectX applications. Let's explore common mesh data structures and how they organize geometric information.

1. Triangle Meshes

The most common type of mesh is the triangle mesh, where the surface of the 3D model is represented by a collection of interconnected triangles.

- **Vertices:** Each vertex stores its position, normal, texture coordinates, and potentially other attributes (e.g., tangents, colors).
- **Faces:** Each face (usually a triangle) defines how vertices are connected to form a polygonal surface.
- **Data Structures:**
  - **Array of Structures:** A simple approach is to store vertices and faces in separate arrays. Each face stores indices into the vertex array to define its constituent vertices.

○ **Indexed Triangle List:** This structure stores vertices in a vertex buffer and faces (triangles) as an indexed triangle list in an index buffer. This allows for efficient rendering and reduces vertex redundancy.

2. Vertex Buffer and Index Buffer

In DirectX, mesh data is typically stored in vertex buffers and index buffers:

- **Vertex Buffer:** Stores the vertex data (position, normal, etc.) in a contiguous block of memory on the GPU.
- **Index Buffer:** Stores the indices that define how the vertices are connected to form triangles. This allows for efficient rendering and reduces vertex redundancy.

3. Advanced Mesh Representations

- **Vertex-Vertex Meshes:** Store a list of neighboring vertices for each vertex. This is useful for operations like smoothing and subdivision.
- **Winged-Edge Data Structure:** A more complex data structure that stores edges, faces, and vertices with pointers connecting them. It provides efficient navigation and manipulation of mesh topology.

- **Half-Edge Data Structure:** A variation of the winged-edge structure that uses half-edges to represent edges, offering more flexibility and efficiency for certain operations.

4. Mesh Attributes

Meshes can store various attributes beyond basic vertex information:

- **Normals:** Surface normals for lighting calculations.
- **Texture Coordinates:** UV coordinates for mapping textures onto the mesh.
- **Tangents and Bitangents:** Used for advanced lighting techniques like normal mapping.
- **Colors:** Vertex colors can be used for blending or other effects.
- **Bone Weights and Indices:** Used for skeletal animation, where vertices are influenced by bones in a skeleton.

5. Choosing the Right Data Structure

The choice of mesh data structure depends on the complexity of your models and the operations you need to perform.

- **Simple Meshes:** An array of structures or an indexed triangle list might suffice for simple static meshes.
- **Complex Meshes:** For complex meshes with dynamic modifications or advanced operations (e.g., subdivision, simulation), more sophisticated data structures like winged-edge or half-edge might be necessary.
- **DirectX Considerations:** DirectX primarily uses vertex buffers and index buffers for rendering. You'll often need to convert your mesh data into this format for efficient rendering.

Moving Forward:

Understanding mesh data structures is crucial for working with 3D models in your DirectX applications. By choosing appropriate data structures and efficiently organizing geometric information, you can optimize rendering performance and enable more complex mesh manipulations. In the next section, we'll explore techniques for optimizing meshes to improve rendering efficiency and reduce memory usage.

Mesh Optimization

3D models can range from simple objects with a few polygons to highly detailed characters and environments with millions of polygons. Optimizing meshes is crucial for achieving efficient rendering and maintaining smooth frame rates, especially in performance-critical applications like games. Let's explore various techniques for optimizing meshes to improve rendering performance and reduce memory usage.

1. Reducing Polygon Count

One of the most effective ways to optimize a mesh is to reduce its polygon count. This involves simplifying the mesh by removing unnecessary polygons without significantly compromising visual fidelity.

- **Decimation:** Algorithms that reduce the number of polygons while preserving the overall shape of the mesh.
- **Level of Detail (LOD):** Creating multiple versions of the mesh with varying levels of detail, using simpler versions when the object is further away from the camera.
- **Manual Simplification:** Using modeling tools to manually remove or simplify polygons in areas that are less visually important.

2. Optimizing Vertex Order

The order in which vertices are stored in the vertex buffer can impact rendering performance.

- **Vertex Caching:** Arrange vertices to maximize vertex cache utilization. Vertices that are used together should be stored close together in memory.
- **Triangle Strips and Fans:** Use triangle strips and fans to reduce the number of indices needed to represent the mesh.

3. Index Optimization

Optimizing the index buffer can improve rendering efficiency.

- **Index Reordering:** Reorder indices to improve vertex cache utilization and reduce the number of vertex transformations.
- **Degenerate Triangles:** Remove degenerate triangles (triangles with zero area) from the mesh.

4. Normal and Tangent Calculations

- **Accurate Normals:** Ensure that vertex normals are calculated correctly to achieve proper lighting and shading.
- **Tangent Space:** Calculate tangent and bitangent vectors for each vertex if you're using normal mapping or other advanced lighting techniques.

5. Texture Coordinate Optimization

- **Efficient UV Mapping:** Create efficient UV maps that minimize texture stretching and distortion.
- **Texture Atlases:** Combine multiple textures into a single texture atlas to reduce texture binding overhead.

6. Mesh Simplification Tools

Various tools and software can assist with mesh optimization:

- **MeshLab:** An open-source tool for mesh processing and optimization.
- **Simplygon:** A commercial tool for automatic mesh simplification and LOD generation.
- **Instant Meshes:** An open-source tool for automatic mesh remeshing and simplification.

7. DirectX Considerations

- **Vertex and Index Buffers:** Use vertex and index buffers efficiently to store and access mesh data.
- **Draw Calls:** Minimize the number of draw calls by batching geometry and using instancing.
- **Resource Management:** Manage resources effectively to avoid unnecessary memory usage and bandwidth consumption.

Moving Forward:

Mesh optimization is a crucial step in the 3D graphics pipeline. By applying these techniques and utilizing available tools, you can significantly improve the performance of your DirectX applications, allowing for more complex and detailed scenes while maintaining smooth frame rates. In the next chapter, we'll delve into special effects, exploring techniques for creating particle systems, billboarding, and post-processing effects.

Animation Basics

Animation is the art of creating the illusion of movement by displaying a sequence of images or frames. In 3D graphics, animation involves changing the properties of objects over time, such as their position, orientation, or shape. This brings characters, environments, and objects to life, creating dynamic and engaging experiences. Let's explore the fundamental concepts of animation in the context of DirectX.

1. Keyframes and Interpolation

- **Keyframes:** Keyframes are specific points in time where you define the desired state of an object (position, rotation, scale, etc.). They act as markers that guide the animation.
- **Interpolation:** The process of calculating the intermediate frames between keyframes. This

creates smooth transitions between different poses or states.

- **Interpolation Techniques:**
  - **Linear Interpolation:** Calculates intermediate values by linearly interpolating between keyframe values.
  - **Spline Interpolation:** Uses curves (splines) to create smoother and more natural transitions between keyframes.

2. Types of Animation

- **Transform Animation:** Changing the position, rotation, or scale of an object over time. This is commonly used for animating object movement, camera paths, and character locomotion.
- **Skeletal Animation:** Animating characters or objects with a skeletal structure. Bones in the skeleton are animated, and the vertices of the mesh are deformed accordingly.
- **Morph Target Animation (Blendshape Animation):** Blending between different predefined shapes (morph targets) of a mesh. This is often used for facial expressions or subtle shape changes.
- **Procedural Animation:** Generating animation based on algorithms or mathematical functions. This can create effects like water ripples, cloth simulations, or particle systems.

3. Animation Data

Animation data can be stored in various formats:

- **Animation Files:** External files (e.g., .fbx, .dae) that store animation data alongside the 3D model.
- **Custom Data Structures:** Define your own data structures in code to store keyframes and animation curves.

4. Implementing Animation in DirectX

- **Loading Animation Data:** Use libraries like Assimp to load animation data from external files.
- **Updating Transformations:** In your update loop, calculate the current animation state based on time and interpolation.
- **Applying Transformations:** Apply the calculated transformations to the object's world matrix before rendering.
- **Skeletal Animation:** Implement skeletal animation by traversing the bone hierarchy, calculating bone transformations, and applying them to the mesh vertices.

5. Animation Techniques

- **Easing:** Control the acceleration and deceleration of animation to create more natural movement.

- **Looping:** Loop animations seamlessly to create continuous movement.
- **Blending:** Blend between different animations to create smooth transitions or combine animations (e.g., walking and waving).

6. DirectX Considerations

- **Frame Rate Independence:** Ensure that animation speed is independent of the frame rate to maintain consistent animation across different systems.
- **Performance:** Optimize animation calculations and data structures to avoid performance bottlenecks.

Moving Forward:

Animation breathes life into your 3D scenes, creating dynamic and engaging experiences. By understanding the principles of animation, loading animation data, and implementing animation techniques in your DirectX applications, you can bring your characters and objects to life. In the next chapter, we'll explore special effects, including particle systems, billboarding, and post-processing techniques.

Chapter 11: Special Effects

Particle Systems

Particle systems are a powerful technique for simulating a wide range of visual effects that are difficult to achieve with traditional rendering methods.[1] They are used to create effects like fire, smoke, explosions, rain, snow, and more.[2] By generating and animating a large number of small particles, you can create the illusion of complex and dynamic phenomena.[3]

1. What are Particle Systems?

A particle system is a collection of individual particles, each with its own properties like position, velocity, color, and size.[4] These particles are generated, animated, and rendered over time to create the desired effect.[5]

Key Components:

- **Emitter:** The source that generates the particles.[6] It defines the rate of emission, initial particle properties, and the area or volume from which particles are emitted.[7]
- **Particle:** A small, typically 2D sprite or 3D point, that represents a single element in the system.[8]

- **Updater:** Updates the properties of the particles over time, such as their position, velocity, color, and size.
- **Renderer:** Renders the particles on the screen, using techniques like billboarding or point sprites.[9]

2. Particle Properties

Particles can have various properties that influence their appearance and behavior:[10]

- **Position:** The location of the particle in 3D space.
- **Velocity:** The direction and speed of the particle's movement.
- **Color:** The color of the particle, which can change over time.[11]
- **Size:** The size of the particle, which can also change over time.
- **Lifetime:** The duration for which the particle exists before being destroyed.
- **Rotation:** The rotation of the particle around its center.
- **Texture:** The texture used to render the particle.

3. Particle System Dynamics

- **Forces:** Apply forces (gravity, wind, etc.) to influence particle movement.[12]

- **Collision Detection:** Detect collisions with other objects or particles to alter their behavior.[13]
- **Fading:** Fade particles in and out over time to create smooth transitions.[14]
- **Color Variation:** Vary the color of particles over time or based on their properties.[15]
- **Size Variation:** Vary the size of particles over time or based on their properties.[16]

4. Implementing Particle Systems in DirectX

- **Particle Structure:** Define a structure in your code to represent a single particle and its properties.
- **Particle Buffer:** Create a buffer to store an array of particles.
- **Emitter:** Implement an emitter that generates new particles with initial properties.[17]
- **Updater:** Implement an update function that updates the properties of all particles each frame.
- **Renderer:** Render the particles using techniques like billboarding or point sprites.[18]

5. Optimization Techniques

- **Instancing:** Use instancing to render multiple particles with a single draw call.
- **Vertex Buffers:** Update particle data directly in vertex buffers to avoid unnecessary data transfers.

- **Compute Shaders:** Utilize compute shaders to perform particle updates on the GPU, taking advantage of parallel processing.[19]

6. Example (Simplified)

C++

```cpp
// Particle structure
struct Particle
{
    XMFLOAT3 position;
    XMFLOAT3 velocity;
    XMFLOAT4 color;
    float size;
    float lifetime;
};

// ... (Create particle buffer, emitter, updater, renderer) ...

// Update particles
void UpdateParticles(float deltaTime)
```

```cpp
{
    for (Particle& particle : particles)
    {
        particle.position += particle.velocity * deltaTime;
        particle.lifetime -= deltaTime;
        // ... (update other properties) ...
    }
}

// Render particles
void RenderParticles()
{
    // ... (Set pipeline state, bind resources) ...
    commandList->DrawInstanced(numParticles, 1, 0, 0);
}
```

Moving Forward:

Particle systems are a versatile tool for creating a wide range of special effects in your DirectX applications.[20] By understanding the core concepts, implementing particle system dynamics, and applying optimization techniques, you can create realistic and visually stunning effects like fire, smoke, explosions, and more.[21] In the next section, we'll explore other special effects techniques, such as billboarding and post-processing.

Billboarding

Billboarding is a clever technique used to create the illusion of 3D objects using flat, 2D sprites. These sprites are oriented to always face the camera, regardless of the camera's position or movement. This creates a convincing effect for objects that are relatively small or distant, where the lack of true 3D geometry is less noticeable.

1. How Billboarding Works

- **Oriented Sprites:** Billboards are essentially 2D images (sprites) that are rotated to face the camera.
- **Vertex Transformation:** The vertices of the billboard are transformed in the vertex shader to align its normal with the view direction.

- **Camera Alignment:** This ensures that the billboard always appears to face the camera, regardless of how the camera moves or rotates.

2. Types of Billboarding

- **World-Oriented Billboards:** The billboard is aligned with the world's up vector (usually the Y-axis). This is useful for objects like trees or smoke plumes that should appear upright regardless of the camera's orientation.
- **View-Oriented Billboards:** The billboard is aligned with the camera's view direction. This is useful for objects like particles or decals that should always face the viewer.
- **Axis-Aligned Billboards:** The billboard is aligned with a specific axis (X, Y, or Z). This can be used for effects like fences or walls.

3. Implementing Billboarding in DirectX

- **Vertex Shader:** The vertex shader is responsible for transforming the billboard vertices to face the camera.
- **Calculate View Direction:** Calculate the view direction in the vertex shader (the vector from the billboard's position to the camera's position).
- **Align Normal:** Align the billboard's normal vector with the view direction.

- **Transform Vertices:** Transform the billboard's vertices based on the aligned normal and the desired billboard type.

4. Optimization Techniques

- **Instancing:** Use instancing to render multiple billboards with a single draw call, especially if they share the same texture.
- **Geometry Shaders:** Geometry shaders can be used to generate billboard geometry on the GPU, reducing CPU overhead.

5. Applications of Billboarding

- **Particle Systems:** Render particles as billboards to create effects like fire, smoke, and explosions.
- **Vegetation:** Render trees, grass, and other foliage as billboards in the distance to improve performance.
- **Special Effects:** Create effects like lens flares, explosions, and decals using billboards.
- **Impostors:** Use billboards as simplified representations of complex objects in the distance.

6. Example (Simplified HLSL Vertex Shader)

High-level shader language

VS_OUTPUT main(VS_INPUT input)

```
{
    // ...


    // Calculate view direction
        float3 viewDir = normalize(cameraPosition -
input.worldPos);


        // Align billboard normal with view direction
(view-oriented billboard)
    float3 billboardNormal = viewDir;


        // ... (Transform billboard vertices based on
billboardNormal) ...

}
```

Moving Forward:

Billboarding is a valuable technique for efficiently
rendering objects that always face the camera. By
understanding the different types of billboarding and
implementing the necessary vertex shader

transformations, you can create a wide range of special effects and optimize the rendering of complex scenes. In the next section, we'll explore post-processing effects, which are applied to the rendered image to enhance its visual quality.

Post-Processing Effects (Bloom, Blur)

Post-processing effects are applied to the rendered image after the 3D scene has been processed by the graphics pipeline. They are used to enhance the visual quality of the final image, creating effects like bloom, blur, color correction, and more. These effects can add realism, atmosphere, and artistic flair to your DirectX applications.

1. What are Post-Processing Effects?

Post-processing effects manipulate the rendered image as a 2D texture, applying various filters and algorithms to achieve the desired visual result. They are typically implemented using shaders and render targets.

Key Concepts:

- **Render Targets:** Post-processing is usually done by rendering the 3D scene to an off-screen render target (texture). This rendered image is then used as input for the post-processing shaders.

- **Shaders:** Post-processing shaders operate on the rendered image, applying effects like blur, bloom, or color grading.
- **Fullscreen Quad:** A common technique is to render a fullscreen quad (two triangles covering the entire screen) and apply the post-processing shader to it.

2. Bloom

Bloom simulates the way bright light bleeds into surrounding areas, creating a soft glow around bright objects. It adds a sense of realism and enhances the visual impact of bright lights and highlights.

- **Implementation:**
    - **Extract Bright Areas:** Separate the bright areas of the image by applying a threshold filter.
    - **Blur:** Blur the extracted bright areas using a Gaussian blur or other blur filter.
    - **Combine:** Combine the blurred bright areas with the original image, creating the bloom effect.

3. Blur

Blurring softens the image, reducing sharp edges and details. It can be used for various effects, such as depth of field, motion blur, and softening shadows.

- **Types of Blur:**
  - **Gaussian Blur:** A common blur technique that uses a Gaussian function to weight the contribution of neighboring pixels.
  - **Box Blur:** A simpler blur that averages the color of neighboring pixels within a box-shaped kernel.
  - **Directional Blur:** Blurs the image in a specific direction, often used for motion blur.
- **Implementation:**
  - **Convolution:** Blurring is typically implemented using convolution, where a kernel (a small matrix of weights) is applied to each pixel in the image.
  - **Multiple Passes:** For stronger blur effects, multiple blur passes can be applied.

4. Other Post-Processing Effects

- **Color Correction:** Adjusting the color balance, saturation, and contrast of the image.
- **Depth of Field:** Simulating the blurring of objects that are out of focus.
- **Motion Blur:** Simulating the blurring of moving objects.

- **Vignette:** Darkening the edges of the image to draw attention to the center.
- **Film Grain:** Adding noise to the image to simulate the look of film.

5. Implementing Post-Processing in DirectX

- **Render to Texture:** Render the 3D scene to an off-screen render target.
- **Create Post-Processing Shaders:** Write HLSL shaders to implement the desired post-processing effects.
- **Render Fullscreen Quad:** Render a fullscreen quad and apply the post-processing shader to it.
- **Multiple Render Targets:** For complex effects, use multiple render targets to store intermediate results.

6. Optimization Techniques

- **Downsampling:** Downsample the image before applying blur to reduce the number of pixels processed.
- **Separable Blur:** Implement Gaussian blur as two separate passes (horizontal and vertical) to reduce the number of texture reads.
- **Shader Optimizations:** Optimize your post-processing shaders to minimize texture fetches and calculations.

Moving Forward:

Post-processing effects are a powerful way to enhance the visual quality of your DirectX applications. By understanding the techniques and implementing various effects like bloom and blur, you can add realism, atmosphere, and artistic style to your 3D scenes. In the next chapter, we'll explore how to build complete applications using DirectX, including game development and simulation.

Skyboxes and Environment Mapping

Skyboxes and environment mapping are techniques used to create the illusion of a surrounding environment in your 3D scenes. They add depth and realism by simulating the reflection of the environment on the surfaces of objects.

1. Skyboxes

A skybox is a large cube that surrounds the scene, with its inner surfaces textured with images representing the sky, distant landscape, or other surrounding environment.

- **Creating the Illusion:** The skybox is rendered first, and then the 3D scene is rendered on top of it. Since the skybox is very large, it appears to be at an infinite distance, creating the illusion of a surrounding environment.

- **Implementation:**
  - ○ **Cubemap Texture:** A skybox typically uses a cubemap texture, which consists of six images representing the six faces of a cube.
  - ○ **Rendering:** Render the skybox cube with depth testing disabled or set to always pass, ensuring it's rendered behind all other objects.
  - ○ **Shader:** In the skybox shader, sample the cubemap texture based on the view direction.

2. Environment Mapping

Environment mapping simulates the reflection of the surrounding environment on the surfaces of objects. It creates a more realistic and immersive experience by making objects appear to reflect their surroundings.

- **Types of Environment Mapping:**
  - ○ **Reflection Mapping:** Reflects the environment directly, creating a mirror-like effect.
  - ○ **Refraction Mapping:** Simulates the bending of light as it passes through a transparent object.

- **Implementation:**
  - **Cubemap Texture:** Environment mapping also typically uses a cubemap texture to represent the surrounding environment.
  - **Shader:** In the object's shader, calculate the reflection vector and use it to sample the cubemap texture.

3. Dynamic Cubemaps

For more dynamic environments, you can generate cubemaps dynamically at runtime.

- **Rendering to Cubemap:** Render the scene from the object's perspective to a cubemap texture.
- **Updating:** Update the cubemap periodically or whenever the environment changes significantly.

4. Optimization Techniques

- **Mipmapping:** Use mipmaps for the cubemap texture to improve performance and reduce aliasing.
- **Pre-filtering:** Pre-filter the cubemap for different roughness levels to optimize specular reflections.

5. Applications

- **Creating Realistic Skies:** Skyboxes are commonly used to create realistic skies and distant environments.
- **Reflecting Environments:** Environment mapping is used to simulate reflections on shiny surfaces like cars, water, and metal objects.
- **Creating Immersive Environments:** Combining skyboxes and environment mapping creates a more immersive and believable 3D world.

6. Example (Simplified HLSL Shader for Environment Mapping)

High-level shader language

```
TextureCube environmentMap : register(t0);

SamplerState sampler0 : register(s0);


float4 main(VS_OUTPUT input) : SV_TARGET
{
    // ...


    float3 reflectDir = reflect(-viewDir, normal);

    float4 reflectedColor = environmentMap.Sample(sampler0, reflectDir);
```

```
// ... (Combine reflectedColor with other lighting
components) ...

}
```

Moving Forward:

Skyboxes and environment mapping are powerful
techniques for creating immersive and realistic 3D
environments. By understanding how to implement these
techniques and utilize cubemap textures effectively, you
can significantly enhance the visual quality of your
DirectX applications. In the next chapter, we'll explore
how to build complete applications, including game
development and simulation.

Chapter 12: Introduction to DirectX 12 Ultimate

DirectX Raytracing (DXR) is a groundbreaking addition to DirectX 12 that brings real-time ray tracing to the forefront of graphics rendering. Unlike traditional rasterization, which approximates how light interacts with objects, ray tracing simulates the physical behavior of light, resulting in incredibly realistic reflections, refractions, shadows, and global illumination. This section delves into the fundamentals of DXR, providing a solid foundation for understanding and implementing this powerful technology.

1. What is Ray Tracing?

Ray tracing is a rendering technique that traces the path of light rays as they interact with objects in a scene. By simulating how light rays bounce, refract, and are absorbed, ray tracing can achieve stunningly accurate and realistic visuals.

- **Casting Rays:** Rays are cast from the camera into the scene, tracing their paths as they intersect objects.

- **Intersection Tests:** Intersection tests are performed to determine if a ray hits an object.
- **Shading Calculations:** If a ray intersects an object, shading calculations are performed to determine the color of the pixel based on the object's material properties, lighting, and other factors.

2. DXR: Ray Tracing in DirectX 12

DXR introduces a new set of APIs and shader types specifically designed for ray tracing. It integrates seamlessly with existing DirectX 12 features, allowing developers to combine ray tracing with traditional rasterization techniques.

- **Acceleration Structures:** DXR utilizes acceleration structures to optimize ray-triangle intersection tests, significantly improving performance.
- **Ray Tracing Pipeline:** DXR introduces a dedicated ray tracing pipeline that operates alongside the rasterization pipeline.
- **Shader Types:** DXR introduces new shader types for ray tracing:
  - **Ray Generation Shaders:** Initiate ray tracing by generating rays.

- Intersection Shaders: Define the geometry of custom procedural primitives.
- Any Hit Shaders: Executed when a ray hits an object, allowing for early termination or special effects.
- Closest Hit Shaders: Executed when a ray hits an object at the closest intersection point, performing shading calculations.
- Miss Shaders: Executed when a ray doesn't hit any object, determining the background color.

3. Acceleration Structures

Acceleration structures are hierarchical data structures that organize scene geometry to optimize ray-triangle intersection tests. DXR uses two levels of acceleration structures:

- **Bottom-Level Acceleration Structures (BLAS):** Represent individual objects or groups of triangles.
- **Top-Level Acceleration Structures (TLAS):** Represent the entire scene, organizing the BLAS.

4. Ray Tracing Pipeline

The DXR ray tracing pipeline operates alongside the rasterization pipeline. It involves the following stages:

- **Ray Generation:** Ray generation shaders generate rays and initiate ray tracing.
- **Traversal:** The ray tracing engine traverses the acceleration structures to find ray-triangle intersections.
- **Shader Execution:** The appropriate shaders (any hit, closest hit, miss) are executed based on the ray's intersection results.
- **Output:** The results of the ray tracing are combined with the rasterized output to produce the final image.

5. Benefits of DXR

- **Realism:** DXR enables real-time rendering of realistic lighting effects, including accurate reflections, refractions, shadows, and global illumination.
- **Performance:** DXR leverages dedicated hardware acceleration on modern GPUs, enabling efficient ray tracing in real-time.
- **Integration:** DXR integrates seamlessly with existing DirectX 12 features, allowing developers to combine ray tracing with rasterization techniques.

6. Applications of DXR

- **Games:** DXR is transforming game graphics, enabling realistic lighting, reflections, and shadows.
- **Simulations:** DXR can be used to simulate the behavior of light in various simulations, such as architectural lighting design or scientific visualizations.
- **Visual Effects:** DXR enables the creation of stunning visual effects, such as realistic water, glass, and other materials.

Moving Forward:

DXR represents a significant advancement in real-time graphics rendering. By understanding the fundamentals of ray tracing, acceleration structures, and the DXR pipeline, you can harness the power of this technology to create stunningly realistic and immersive 3D experiences. In the following sections, we'll delve deeper into DXR, exploring how to build acceleration structures, write ray tracing shaders, and integrate ray tracing into your DirectX applications.

Raytracing Pipeline

The DirectX Raytracing (DXR) pipeline is a specialized pipeline dedicated to handling ray tracing operations. It works in conjunction with the traditional rasterization pipeline to produce the final rendered image.

Understanding the flow of data and execution within the ray tracing pipeline is crucial for effectively implementing ray tracing effects in your DirectX applications.

1. Ray Generation: The Starting Point

The ray tracing journey begins with the **Ray Generation Shader**. This shader is responsible for:

- **Generating Rays:** It defines the origin and direction of rays that are cast into the scene. These rays can originate from the camera (for primary rays) or from other objects in the scene (for secondary rays, like reflections or shadows).
- **Initializing Payload:** Each ray carries a payload, which is a user-defined data structure that stores information about the ray and its interactions with the scene. The ray generation shader initializes this payload with relevant data.
- **Calling** TraceRay(): The shader calls the TraceRay() function to initiate ray traversal. This function takes the ray's origin, direction, and payload as input.

2. Traversal: Navigating the Scene

Once TraceRay() is called, the DXR ray tracing engine takes over, performing the following steps:

- **Acceleration Structure Traversal:** The engine traverses the acceleration structures (BLAS and TLAS) to efficiently find intersections between the ray and the scene geometry.
- **Intersection Tests:** It performs ray-triangle intersection tests to determine if the ray hits any triangles in the scene.

3. Shader Execution: Handling Intersections

Based on the results of the traversal and intersection tests, the ray tracing engine executes different shader types:

- **Any Hit Shader (Optional):** If an intersection is found, the Any Hit Shader (if present) is executed. This shader can be used for effects like alpha testing or early ray termination.
- **Closest Hit Shader:** If the ray hits an object at the closest intersection point, the Closest Hit Shader is executed. This shader performs the core shading calculations, determining the color of the pixel based on the object's material properties, lighting, and other factors.
- **Miss Shader:** If the ray doesn't hit any object in the scene, the Miss Shader is executed. This shader typically determines the background color or environment contribution.

4. Shader Interaction and Payload

- **Payload Modification:** Shaders (Any Hit, Closest Hit) can modify the ray's payload to store information about the intersection, such as the hit point, surface normal, or material properties. This information can be used for subsequent calculations or passed to other shaders.
- **Spawning New Rays:** Shaders can spawn new rays to simulate effects like reflections, refractions, or shadows. These new rays are traced recursively, and their results contribute to the final pixel color.

5. Output and Integration

- **Returning to Ray Generation Shader:** After the ray tracing is complete, the TraceRay() function returns control to the Ray Generation Shader.
- **Accessing Payload:** The Ray Generation Shader can access the final payload of the ray, which contains the accumulated information from the ray's journey through the scene.
- **Combining with Rasterization:** The output of the ray tracing pipeline is typically combined with the output of the rasterization pipeline to produce the final rendered image.

6. Key Considerations

- **Performance:** The efficiency of the ray tracing pipeline heavily relies on the quality of the acceleration structures and the complexity of the shaders.
- **Recursion:** Recursive ray tracing can be computationally expensive, so it's important to manage the depth of recursion and optimize shader code.
- **Debugging:** Debugging ray tracing shaders can be challenging. Utilize debugging tools and techniques to identify and resolve issues.

Moving Forward:

Understanding the ray tracing pipeline is crucial for effectively implementing ray tracing effects in your DirectX applications. By grasping the roles of the different shader types, the traversal process, and the interaction with the payload, you can create realistic and immersive 3D scenes with accurate lighting, shadows, and reflections. In the following sections, we'll explore how to build acceleration structures, write ray tracing shaders, and integrate ray tracing into your DirectX applications.

Implementing Basic Raytracing Effects

Now that you have a grasp of DXR fundamentals and the ray tracing pipeline, let's explore how to implement some basic ray tracing effects: reflections and shadows. These effects can significantly enhance the realism of your scenes by accurately simulating how light interacts with objects.

1. Reflections: Mirroring the World

Reflections occur when light bounces off a surface. To implement reflections with DXR:

- **Closest Hit Shader:** In the closest hit shader of the reflective object, calculate the reflection vector based on the incoming ray direction and the surface normal.
- **Spawn a Reflection Ray:** Use the TraceRay() function to spawn a new ray with the calculated reflection direction.
- **Recursive Tracing:** The ray tracing engine will trace this reflection ray recursively, potentially hitting other objects and generating more reflections.
- **Combine Results:** In the original closest hit shader, combine the color contribution from the reflection ray with the object's own color and lighting.

Example (Simplified HLSL Closest Hit Shader):

High-level shader language

```
float4        main(RayPayload        payload,        in
BuiltInTriangleIntersectionAttributes        attr)        :
SV_TARGET
{
    // ... (Calculate surface normal and other properties) ...


    // Calculate reflection vector
        float3 reflectionDir = reflect(payload.direction,
normal);


    // Spawn a reflection ray
    RayDesc reflectionRay;
    reflectionRay.Origin = hitPosition;
    reflectionRay.Direction = reflectionDir;
    RayPayload reflectionPayload = { float4(0, 0, 0, 1) };
// Initialize payload
    TraceRay(scene, RAY_FLAG_NONE, 0xFF, 0, 1, 0,
reflectionRay, reflectionPayload);
```

```
    // Combine reflection color with other lighting
components

        float4  finalColor  =  material.diffuseColor  *
lightContribution + reflectionPayload.color;


    return finalColor;

}
```

2. Shadows: Casting Darkness

Shadows occur when an object blocks light from
reaching another object. To implement shadows with
DXR:

- **Closest Hit Shader:** In the closest hit shader of
  the object being shaded, cast a shadow ray from
  the hit point towards the light source.
- **Trace Shadow Ray:** Use TraceRay() to trace the
  shadow ray.
- **Check for Intersection:** If the shadow ray
  intersects any object before reaching the light
  source, the hit point is in shadow.
- **Adjust Lighting:** If the hit point is in shadow,
  reduce or eliminate the contribution of the light
  source to the final color.

Example (Simplified HLSL Closest Hit Shader):

High-level shader language

```
float4 main(RayPayload payload, in
BuiltInTriangleIntersectionAttributes attr) :
SV_TARGET
{
    // ... (Calculate surface normal and other properties) ...


    // Cast a shadow ray towards the light source
    RayDesc shadowRay;
    shadowRay.Origin = hitPosition;
        shadowRay.Direction = normalize(lightPosition -
    hitPosition);
    RayPayload shadowPayload = { float4(0, 0, 0, 1) };
        TraceRay(scene, RAY_FLAG_NONE, 0xFF, 0, 1, 0,
    shadowRay, shadowPayload);


    // Check for shadow
        float shadowFactor = shadowPayload.color.a > 0.0f ?
    0.5f : 1.0f; // Reduce light contribution if in shadow
```

```
// Calculate lighting with shadow factor

    float4 finalColor = material.diffuseColor *
lightContribution * shadowFactor;


    return finalColor;

}
```

3. Combining Effects

You can combine reflections and shadows to create even more realistic scenes. For example, a reflective object can reflect the shadows cast by other objects.

4. Optimization Considerations

- **Ray Flags:** Use ray flags (e.g., RAY_FLAG_SKIP_CLOSEST_HIT_SHADER) to optimize ray tracing by skipping unnecessary shader executions.
- **Recursion Depth:** Limit the recursion depth for reflection rays to avoid performance issues.
- **Shader Complexity:** Optimize your shaders to minimize calculations and texture fetches.

Moving Forward:

Implementing basic ray tracing effects like reflections and shadows can significantly enhance the realism of your 3D scenes. By understanding how to cast rays, perform intersection tests, and adjust lighting based on ray tracing results, you can create stunning visuals that accurately simulate the behavior of light. As you explore more advanced ray tracing techniques, you'll discover even more ways to create realistic and immersive 3D worlds.

Variable Rate Shading (VRS)

Variable Rate Shading (VRS) is a powerful rendering technique introduced in DirectX 12 that allows developers to control the shading rate on a per-pixel basis. This means that different parts of the screen can be shaded with varying levels of detail, optimizing performance by reducing the computational load in areas where full detail isn't necessary.

1. Traditional Shading vs. VRS

- **Traditional Shading:** In traditional rendering, every pixel on the screen is shaded with the same level of detail, regardless of its importance or visual complexity.

- **VRS:** VRS allows you to vary the shading rate, shading some pixels individually and others in groups (2x2, 4x4). This enables you to focus shading power where it matters most.

2. How VRS Works

- **Shading Rate:** The shading rate determines how many pixels are processed by a single invocation of the pixel shader.
- **Controlling Shading Rate:** You can control the shading rate using various methods:
    - **Tier 1:** Coarse shading rates (1x1, 2x2, 4x4) are specified per draw call.
    - **Tier 2:** Finer-grained control using a shading rate image, which defines the shading rate for each pixel on the screen.

3. Benefits of VRS

- **Performance Improvement:** By reducing the shading rate in less important areas, you can significantly improve rendering performance, especially in complex scenes.
- **Improved Frame Rates:** Higher frame rates can be achieved without sacrificing visual quality in critical areas.
- **Foveated Rendering:** VRS enables foveated rendering, where the area around the user's gaze

is rendered with higher detail, while peripheral areas are shaded with lower detail.

4. Use Cases for VRS

- **Areas with Low Detail:** Reduce the shading rate in areas with low visual detail, such as distant objects or backgrounds.
- **Motion Blur:** Reduce the shading rate in areas affected by motion blur, as the details are already less perceptible.
- **Foveated Rendering:** Implement foveated rendering in VR applications to optimize performance and focus rendering power on the areas where the user is looking.

5. Implementing VRS in DirectX 12

- **Tier 1:**
  - D3D12_GRAPHICS_PIPELINE_STATE_DESC: Set the VariableRateShadingRate member in the pipeline state description structure.
  - ID3D12GraphicsCommandList::SetShadingRate: Use this method to set the shading rate for subsequent draw calls.
- **Tier 2:**
  - **Shading Rate Image:** Create a shading rate image resource to define the per-pixel shading rates.

- ○ ID3D12GraphicsCommandList::RSSetSh adingRateImage: Bind the shading rate image to the rendering pipeline.

6. Considerations

- **Visual Quality:** Carefully choose shading rates to avoid noticeable visual artifacts.
- **Hardware Support:** VRS requires hardware support. Check for feature support before using it.
- **Content Appropriateness:** VRS is not suitable for all types of content. For example, it might not be ideal for scenes with sharp edges or fine details.

Moving Forward:

Variable Rate Shading is a valuable tool for optimizing performance in your DirectX 12 applications. By understanding how to control the shading rate and apply it to different areas of the screen, you can achieve significant performance gains without sacrificing overall visual quality. As you explore more advanced rendering techniques, consider how VRS can be integrated to further enhance the efficiency of your applications.

Part IV: Building Applications

Chapter 13: Game Development with DirectX

Game Loop Architecture

At the core of every game lies the game loop - a continuously running cycle that drives the game's logic, rendering, and interaction. It's the engine that keeps the game alive, processing input, updating the game world, and rendering frames to the screen. Understanding game loop architecture is crucial for creating responsive, efficient, and engaging games with DirectX.

1. The Basic Game Loop

A typical game loop consists of three main phases:

- **Process Input:** Gather input from the player, such as keyboard, mouse, or gamepad actions.
- **Update Game State:** Update the game world based on the input and the passage of time. This includes updating object positions, handling physics, AI, and game logic.
- **Render Frame:** Render the game scene to the screen, displaying the updated game world to the player.

Simplified Code Example:

```cpp
C++

while (true)

{

    ProcessInput();

    UpdateGameState();

    RenderFrame();

}
```

2. Variations and Considerations

- **Fixed Timestep:** Use a fixed timestep to ensure consistent game logic updates, regardless of frame rate fluctuations. This involves dividing time into fixed intervals and updating the game state in discrete steps.
- **Variable Timestep:** Update the game state based on the actual time elapsed since the last frame. This can provide smoother animation and movement but requires careful handling of time-dependent calculations.
- **Delta Time:** Calculate the time elapsed since the last frame (delta time) and use it in your update calculations to ensure frame rate independence.

- **Game State Management:** Organize your game state into logical components (player, enemies, objects, etc.) for easier management and updates.

3. Advanced Game Loop Architectures

- **Multithreading:** Utilize multithreading to parallelize tasks like physics calculations, AI processing, or audio updates, improving performance on multi-core processors.
- **Data-Oriented Design:** Organize game data in a way that optimizes memory access and cache utilization, improving performance.
- **Event-Driven Architecture:** Use an event-driven system to handle game events and decouple different parts of the game logic.

4. DirectX Integration

- **Command Queues and Lists:** Utilize DirectX 12's command queues and lists to efficiently submit rendering commands to the GPU.
- **Synchronization:** Use fences and other synchronization mechanisms to ensure proper timing and avoid race conditions between CPU and GPU operations.
- **Frame Rate Management:** Implement techniques like vsync or frame rate limiting to control the rendering speed and avoid screen tearing.

5. Example with DirectX 12 (Simplified)

```cpp
C++

while (running)
{
    // Process input
    // ...

    // Update game state
    Update(deltaTime);

    // Render frame
        PopulateCommandList(); // Record rendering commands

        commandQueue->ExecuteCommandLists(1, commandList.GetAddressOf());

    swapChain->Present(1, 0); // Present the frame

    // Synchronization and frame rate management
```

```
    // ...

}
```

6. Game Loop Best Practices

- **Efficiency:** Optimize your game loop to minimize CPU and GPU overhead, ensuring smooth frame rates.
- **Responsiveness:** Process input and update the game state frequently to maintain responsiveness.
- **Frame Rate Independence:** Use delta time and other techniques to ensure that game logic and animation are independent of the frame rate.
- **Maintainability:** Structure your game loop code for clarity and maintainability, making it easier to debug and extend.

Moving Forward:

The game loop is the driving force behind your DirectX games. By understanding its architecture, implementing variations like fixed or variable timesteps, and integrating it effectively with DirectX 12, you can create responsive, efficient, and engaging game experiences. In the next section, we'll explore input handling, a crucial aspect of game development that allows players to interact with your game world.

Input Handling

Input handling is a fundamental aspect of game development, enabling players to interact with your game world and control the action. It involves capturing input from various devices, such as keyboards, mice, and gamepads, and translating those inputs into meaningful actions within the game. Let's explore how to implement effective input handling in your DirectX games.

1. Input Devices and Events

- **Keyboard:** Capture key presses and releases to trigger actions like movement, jumping, or firing weapons.
- **Mouse:** Capture mouse movements, button clicks, and scroll wheel events for camera control, object selection, or menu navigation.
- **Gamepad:** Capture button presses, joystick movements, and trigger pulls for a more immersive and console-like experience.
- **Other Devices:** Consider supporting other input devices, such as touchscreens or motion sensors, depending on your game's platform and target audience.

2. Input APIs

- **Windows Message Loop:** The traditional way to handle input in Windows applications is through the message loop. You can capture and process WM_KEYDOWN, WM_KEYUP, WM_MOUSEMOVE, and other input messages.

- **DirectInput:** DirectInput is a DirectX API specifically designed for handling input from various devices. It provides a more direct and low-level approach to input capture.
- **XInput:** XInput is a newer API that focuses on handling input from Xbox controllers. It provides a standardized way to access gamepad input.
- **Raw Input:** Raw Input is a low-level API that provides access to raw input data from devices, bypassing any filtering or processing.

3. Input Handling Techniques

- **Polling:** Periodically check the state of input devices to detect changes. This is a simple approach but can be less responsive for rapid input changes.
- **Events:** Use event-driven input handling, where input events (key presses, mouse clicks) are triggered and handled as they occur. This provides more immediate response to input.
- **Input Mapping:** Map input events to specific game actions. This allows you to customize controls and support different input devices.

- **Input Buffering:** Store input events in a buffer to handle input that occurs between frames, ensuring smooth and consistent response.

4. Implementing Input Handling in DirectX

- **Choose an API:** Select an appropriate input API based on your game's needs and target platform.
- **Initialize Input Devices:** Initialize the input devices you want to use (keyboard, mouse, gamepad).
- **Capture Input Events:** Capture input events in your game loop using the chosen API.
- **Translate Input to Actions:** Map the captured input events to specific game actions (e.g., move player, fire weapon).
- **Apply Actions:** Update the game state based on the triggered actions.

5. Example (Simplified Keyboard Input with Windows Message Loop)

C++

```
// In your message handling function (WndProc)

case WM_KEYDOWN:

  if (wParam == 'W')

    player.MoveForward();
```

```
break;

case WM_KEYUP:
  if (wParam == 'W')
    player.StopMoving();
  break;
```

6. Input Handling Best Practices

- **Responsiveness:** Handle input events promptly to ensure a responsive and engaging game experience.
- **Customization:** Allow players to customize controls to their preferences.
- **Input Buffering:** Use input buffering to handle input that occurs between frames.
- **Dead Zones:** Implement dead zones for analog inputs (joysticks) to prevent unintended movement.
- **Input Smoothing:** Apply input smoothing to reduce jitter and create smoother movement.

Moving Forward:

Effective input handling is essential for creating interactive and engaging games. By understanding different input devices, APIs, and techniques, you can capture player actions and translate them into meaningful game events. As you develop your DirectX games, consider how to implement input handling that is responsive, customizable, and intuitive for your players. In the next section, we'll explore collision detection, a crucial aspect of game physics that allows objects to interact with each other in a realistic way.

Collision Detection

Collision detection is a fundamental aspect of game physics, enabling objects in your game world to interact with each other realistically. It involves determining if two or more objects are intersecting or colliding, triggering actions like bouncing, triggering events, or preventing objects from passing through each other. Let's explore common collision detection techniques and how to implement them in your DirectX games.

1. Bounding Volumes

Bounding volumes are simplified geometric shapes that enclose objects. They are used to approximate the shape of objects for efficient collision detection. Common bounding volumes include:

- **Axis-Aligned Bounding Boxes (AABBs):** Boxes that are aligned with the world coordinate axes. They are simple to represent and test for collisions but can be less accurate for irregularly shaped objects.
- **Bounding Spheres:** Spheres that enclose the object. They are also relatively simple to represent and test for collisions.
- **Oriented Bounding Boxes (OBBs):** Boxes that can be oriented in any direction. They provide a tighter fit for many objects but are more complex to test for collisions.
- **Capsules:** Cylinders with hemispherical ends. They are useful for representing elongated objects.

2. Collision Detection Algorithms

- **AABB-AABB Collision:** Check if the minimum and maximum extents of two AABBs overlap on all three axes.
- **Sphere-Sphere Collision:** Check if the distance between the centers of two spheres is less than the sum of their radii.
- **AABB-Sphere Collision:** Find the closest point on the AABB to the sphere's center and check if the distance between those points is less than the sphere's radius.

- **OBB-OBB Collision:** More complex algorithms are required to test for collisions between OBBs, often involving separating axis tests.
- **Triangle-Triangle Collision:** For more precise collision detection, you can test for collisions between individual triangles in the meshes of the objects.

3. Collision Response

Once a collision is detected, you need to implement collision response to determine how the objects should react.

- **Separation:** Move the objects apart to resolve the collision.
- **Bouncing:** Calculate the new velocities of the objects after the collision, simulating bouncing or deflection.
- **Triggering Events:** Trigger game events based on the collision, such as playing a sound, damaging an object, or ending the game.

4. Implementing Collision Detection in DirectX

- **Choose Bounding Volumes:** Select appropriate bounding volumes for your objects based on their shapes and the desired accuracy.

- **Update Bounding Volumes:** Update the bounding volumes each frame to reflect the objects' current positions and orientations.
- **Perform Collision Tests:** Implement collision detection algorithms to check for intersections between bounding volumes.
- **Implement Collision Response:** Handle collisions by separating objects, applying forces, or triggering events.

5. Optimization Techniques

- **Spatial Partitioning:** Divide the game world into smaller regions (e.g., using grids, octrees, or BSP trees) to reduce the number of collision tests needed.
- **Broad Phase and Narrow Phase:** Use a broad phase to quickly identify potential collisions and then a narrow phase to perform more precise collision tests.
- **Caching:** Cache collision information to avoid redundant calculations.

6. Example (Simplified AABB-AABB Collision)

```cpp
C++

bool AABBCollision(const AABB& a, const AABB& b)
{
```

```
    if (a.max.x < b.min.x || a.min.x > b.max.x) return
false;

    if (a.max.y < b.min.y || a.min.y > b.max.y) return
false;

  if (a.max.z < b.min.z || a.min.z > b.max.z) return false;

  return true;

}
```

Moving Forward:

Collision detection is a crucial component of game physics, enabling realistic interactions between objects in your game world. By understanding different bounding volumes, collision detection algorithms, and collision response techniques, you can create engaging and immersive game experiences. As you develop your DirectX games, consider how to implement efficient and accurate collision detection to enhance the realism and interactivity of your game world. In the next section, we'll explore how to build a simple 3D game using the concepts we've covered so far.

Building a Simple 3D Game

It's time to put all the knowledge you've gained throughout this book into practice and build a simple 3D game using DirectX 12. This project will solidify your understanding of the core concepts and provide a foundation for creating more complex and engaging games in the future.

1. Game Concept

For this example, let's create a simple 3D game where the player controls a cube and navigates a basic environment. The player can move the cube using the keyboard, and the camera follows the cube's movement.

2. Core Components

- **Game Loop:** Implement a game loop with input processing, game state updates, and rendering.
- **Input Handling:** Handle keyboard input to control the player's movement.
- **3D Model:** Load a simple cube model or create one programmatically.
- **Camera:** Implement a third-person camera that follows the player's cube.
- **Rendering:** Render the 3D scene, including the player's cube and the environment.

3. Implementation Steps

- **Initialization:**
  - Initialize DirectX 12 (device, command queue, swap chain, etc.).
  - Create resources (vertex buffer, index buffer, textures).
  - Load the 3D model for the player's cube.
  - Initialize the camera.
- **Game Loop:**
  - **Process Input:** Capture keyboard input (W, A, S, D) for movement.
  - **Update Game State:**
    - Update the player's cube position based on the input.
    - Update the camera's position to follow the player.
  - **Render Frame:**
    - Clear the render target and depth-stencil buffer.
    - Set the rendering pipeline state.
    - Bind resources (vertex buffer, index buffer, textures).
    - Set constant buffers (world matrix, view matrix, projection matrix).
    - Draw the player's cube.
    - Present the frame to the screen.

4. Adding Features

Once you have the basic game running, you can add more features to make it more engaging:

- **Environment:** Create a simple environment with basic shapes or load a pre-made environment model.
- **Collision Detection:** Implement collision detection to prevent the player from moving through walls or other objects.
- **Simple Gameplay:** Add a goal or objective, such as collecting items or reaching a specific location.
- **Basic AI:** Implement simple AI for enemies or other interactive objects.
- **Sound Effects:** Add sound effects for actions like movement, jumping, or collisions.

5. Code Example (Simplified)

```
C++

// ... (Initialization) ...


while (running)

{

    // Process input
```

```
if (GetAsyncKeyState('W') & 0x8000)

    player.MoveForward(deltaTime);

// ... (Handle other movement keys) ...


// Update game state

player.Update(deltaTime);

camera.Update(player.GetPosition());


// Render frame

    // ... (Clear render targets, set pipeline state, bind
resources) ...


commandList->DrawIndexedInstanced(cube.GetIndexC
ount(), 1, 0, 0, 0); // Draw the cube

    // ... (Present frame) ...

}
```

6. Tips for Building Games with DirectX

- **Start Simple:** Begin with a basic game concept and gradually add features.
- **Modular Design:** Break down your game into smaller, manageable modules.
- **Reuse Code:** Create reusable components and functions to avoid code duplication.
- **Debugging:** Utilize debugging tools (Visual Studio debugger, PIX) to identify and fix errors.
- **Performance Optimization:** Apply optimization techniques to ensure smooth frame rates.
- **Game Engines:** Consider using game engines like Unreal Engine or Unity, which provide higher-level abstractions and tools for game development.

Moving Forward:

Building a simple 3D game with DirectX 12 is a rewarding experience that solidifies your understanding of the core concepts and provides a foundation for future game development projects. As you explore more advanced techniques and features, you can create increasingly complex and engaging games. In the next chapter, we'll delve into simulation and visualization, exploring how DirectX can be used for applications beyond gaming.

Chapter 14: Simulation and Visualization

Data visualization is the art and science of transforming raw data into visual representations, making it easier to understand, analyze, and communicate complex information.[1] It leverages the human brain's innate ability to process visual information, revealing patterns, trends, and insights that might otherwise remain hidden in spreadsheets or databases.[2] In this section, we'll explore various data visualization techniques and how DirectX can be used to create compelling and interactive visualizations.

1. Choosing the Right Visualization

The choice of visualization technique depends on the type of data you want to represent and the insights you want to convey.

- **Categorical Data:**
    - **Bar Charts:** Compare values across different categories.[3]
    - **Pie Charts:** Show proportions of a whole.[4]

- o **Stacked Bar Charts:** Compare contributions of different categories to a total.[5]
- **Numerical Data:**
  - o **Line Charts:** Show trends over time or across a continuous variable.[6]
  - o **Scatter Plots:** Visualize relationships between two variables.[7]
  - o **Histograms:** Show the distribution of a single variable.[8]
- **Hierarchical Data:**
  - o **Treemaps:** Visualize hierarchical data as nested rectangles.[9]
  - o **Dendrograms:** Represent hierarchical relationships as tree-like diagrams.[10]
- **Geospatial Data:**
  - o **Maps:** Display data on a geographical map.[11]
  - o **Choropleth Maps:** Use color variations to represent data values across different regions.
- **Network Data:**
  - o **Network Diagrams:** Visualize relationships between entities as nodes and connections.[12]
  - o **Force-Directed Graphs:** Layout nodes based on forces of attraction and repulsion.[13]

2. DirectX for Data Visualization

DirectX provides a powerful platform for creating interactive and high-performance data visualizations.

- **2D and 3D Graphics:** Utilize Direct2D or Direct3D to render charts, graphs, and other visual elements.[14]
- **Shaders:** Leverage HLSL shaders to create custom visual effects and dynamic data representations.[15]
- **GPU Acceleration:** Take advantage of GPU acceleration for fast and efficient rendering of large datasets.
- **User Interaction:** Handle mouse and keyboard input to enable interactive exploration of data.

3. Visualization Techniques with DirectX

- **Dynamic Charts and Graphs:** Create animated and interactive charts and graphs that respond to user input or data changes.
- **3D Scatter Plots:** Visualize data points in 3D space, allowing users to rotate and explore the data from different perspectives.[16]
- **Data-Driven Textures:** Use data to generate textures, creating visualizations that map data values to colors or patterns.

- **Particle Systems:** Represent data points as particles, using particle system dynamics to visualize data flow or relationships.
- **Virtual Reality (VR) Visualizations:** Immerse users in data using VR, enabling them to explore and interact with data in a 3D environment.[17]

4. Best Practices

- **Clarity and Simplicity:** Focus on clear and concise visual representations that effectively communicate the key insights.[18]
- **Appropriate Chart Type:** Choose the right chart type for the data and the message you want to convey.
- **Color Schemes:** Use color strategically to highlight important data points or patterns.[19]
- **Interactivity:** Enable user interaction to allow exploration and deeper understanding of the data.[20]
- **Performance:** Optimize rendering and data processing for smooth and responsive visualizations.

5. Example (Simplified 3D Scatter Plot with DirectX)

```C++

// ... (Initialize DirectX, create resources) ...
```

```cpp
// Render data points as spheres

for (const DataPoint& point : data)

{

    // Set world matrix based on data point coordinates

                    XMMATRIX       worldMatrix       =
XMMatrixTranslation(point.x, point.y, point.z);


    // ... (Set pipeline state, bind resources) ...


    // Draw sphere

commandList->DrawIndexedInstanced(sphere.GetIndex
Count(), 1, 0, 0, 0);

}


// ... (Present frame) ...
```

Moving Forward:

Data visualization is a powerful tool for understanding and communicating complex information.[21] By leveraging DirectX's graphics capabilities and applying effective visualization techniques, you can create compelling and interactive visualizations that bring data to life. As you explore this field, consider how to combine DirectX with data analysis and processing techniques to develop innovative and insightful visualizations. In the next section, we'll explore how to use DirectX for real-time simulation, bringing physics and other dynamic systems into your applications.

Real-time Simulation with DirectX

Real-time simulation involves modeling and visualizing dynamic systems that change over time, such as physics, fluid dynamics, or artificial life. DirectX provides a powerful platform for creating interactive and visually compelling real-time simulations, leveraging the GPU's parallel processing capabilities to accelerate computations and render dynamic visuals.

1. Simulation Techniques

- **Physics Simulation:** Simulate the movement and interaction of objects according to physical laws, including gravity, collisions, and forces.

- **Fluid Dynamics:** Simulate the behavior of fluids like water, smoke, or fire, creating realistic liquid effects, smoke plumes, or fire propagation.
- **Cloth Simulation:** Simulate the movement and draping of cloth, creating realistic garments or fabric animations.
- **Crowd Simulation:** Simulate the movement and behavior of crowds, creating realistic pedestrian flows or group interactions.
- **Artificial Life:** Simulate the behavior of artificial creatures or ecosystems, creating virtual worlds with emergent behavior.

2. DirectX for Simulation

DirectX offers several features that are beneficial for real-time simulation:

- **GPU Acceleration:** Utilize DirectCompute or compute shaders to perform simulation calculations on the GPU, taking advantage of parallel processing for increased performance.
- **Data Structures:** Use DirectX buffers and textures to store and access simulation data efficiently.
- **Interoperability:** Combine simulation results with rendering techniques in Direct3D to visualize the simulation dynamically.

- **User Interaction:** Handle input to allow users to interact with the simulation and influence its behavior.

3. Implementing Simulations with DirectX

- **Choose a Simulation Technique:** Select a simulation technique based on the type of system you want to simulate.
- **Design Data Structures:** Define data structures to represent the entities and properties of the simulation.
- **Implement Simulation Logic:** Implement the core simulation algorithms, often using compute shaders or DirectCompute.
- **Visualize the Simulation:** Render the simulation results using Direct3D, mapping simulation data to visual elements.
- **Handle User Interaction:** Allow users to interact with the simulation through input devices.

4. Optimization Techniques

- **Data Parallelism:** Exploit data parallelism by processing multiple simulation elements concurrently on the GPU.
- **Algorithm Optimization:** Optimize simulation algorithms for GPU execution, minimizing data

dependencies and maximizing parallel processing.

- **Memory Access:** Optimize memory access patterns to reduce cache misses and improve data throughput.

5. Example (Simplified Physics Simulation)

C++

```
// ... (Initialize DirectX, create resources) ...


// Update particle positions in a compute shader

computeShader.Dispatch(numParticles                        /
threadsPerGroup, 1, 1);


// Render particles using Direct3D

// ...


// ... (Present frame) ...
```

6. Applications of Real-time Simulation

- **Games:** Create realistic physics, fluid effects, and character animations in games.
- **Scientific Visualization:** Visualize scientific data and simulations, such as fluid flow, weather patterns, or molecular dynamics.
- **Training and Education:** Develop interactive simulations for training purposes, such as flight simulators or medical simulations.
- **Engineering and Design:** Simulate and visualize engineering systems, such as airflow over an aircraft wing or structural stress analysis.

Moving Forward:

Real-time simulation with DirectX empowers you to create dynamic and interactive virtual worlds. By combining simulation techniques with DirectX's graphics capabilities, you can visualize complex systems, explore emergent behavior, and develop applications that range from realistic games to scientific visualizations and training simulations. As you delve deeper into this field, consider how to leverage the power of the GPU to accelerate simulations and create compelling interactive experiences.

Example: Building a Physics Simulation

Let's dive into a practical example of building a real-time physics simulation using DirectX. We'll create a scene with multiple spheres falling under the influence of gravity and colliding with each other and the ground. This example will demonstrate how to combine physics calculations with DirectX rendering to visualize a dynamic system.

1. Setting Up the Scene

- **Initialization:** Initialize DirectX 12 (device, command queue, swap chain, etc.).
- **Scene Objects:** Create an array of spheres, each represented by:
    - **Position:** 3D vector representing the sphere's position.
    - **Velocity:** 3D vector representing the sphere's velocity.
    - **Radius:** The radius of the sphere.
- **Ground Plane:** Define a plane that represents the ground.

2. Physics Simulation

- **Update Loop:** In the game loop's update phase, perform the following for each sphere:
    - **Apply Gravity:** Update the sphere's velocity by adding the acceleration due to gravity.
    - **Update Position:** Update the sphere's position based on its velocity.

- ○ **Collision Detection:**
  - ■ **Sphere-Ground Collision:** Check if the sphere intersects with the ground plane. If it does, resolve the collision by adjusting its position and reflecting its velocity.
  - ■ **Sphere-Sphere Collision:** Check for collisions between pairs of spheres. If a collision occurs, resolve it by adjusting their positions and applying impulses to change their velocities.

3. Rendering

- **Direct3D Rendering:** Use Direct3D to render the spheres and the ground plane.
- **Update World Matrices:** Update the world matrix of each sphere based on its simulated position.
- **Draw Calls:** Issue draw calls to render the spheres and the ground plane.

4. DirectX Considerations

- **Compute Shaders:** Consider using compute shaders to perform the physics calculations on the GPU, taking advantage of parallel processing for increased performance.

- **Data Structures:** Use DirectX buffers to store and access the sphere data efficiently.
- **Synchronization:** Ensure proper synchronization between the physics simulation and rendering using fences or other synchronization mechanisms.

5. Code Example (Simplified)

C++

```cpp
// ... (Initialization) ...


// Update loop

void Update(float deltaTime)

{

    for (Sphere& sphere : spheres)

    {

        // Apply gravity

        sphere.velocity.y -= gravity * deltaTime;


        // Update position

        sphere.position += sphere.velocity * deltaTime;
```

```cpp
// Sphere-ground collision
if (sphere.position.y - sphere.radius < 0.0f)
{
    sphere.position.y = sphere.radius;
        sphere.velocity.y *= -restitution; // Reflect velocity
}


// Sphere-sphere collision
for (Sphere& other : spheres)
{
    if (&sphere != &other) // Don't check collision with itself
    {
        // ... (Check for collision and resolve) ...
    }
}
}
```

```
}
```

```
// Render spheres

// ...
```

6. Enhancements and Extensions

- **More Complex Objects:** Extend the simulation to handle different shapes, such as cubes or meshes.
- **Forces and Constraints:** Add support for other forces (wind, friction) and constraints (joints, springs).
- **User Interaction:** Allow the user to interact with the simulation, such as applying forces to objects or creating new objects.

Moving Forward:

Building a physics simulation with DirectX provides a practical example of how to combine simulation logic with real-time rendering. By understanding the core concepts of physics simulation, collision detection, and DirectX integration, you can create dynamic and interactive experiences that showcase the power of real-time simulation. As you explore further, consider how to apply these techniques to other simulation domains, such as fluid dynamics or cloth simulation, to create even more compelling and realistic virtual worlds.

Chapter 15: Beyond the Basics

Further DirectX Features (DirectCompute, DirectML)

While Direct3D forms the core of DirectX graphics, the API suite offers much more than just rendering 3D scenes. DirectX also provides powerful tools for general-purpose GPU programming and hardware-accelerated machine learning. In this section, we'll explore two such features: DirectCompute and DirectML.

1. DirectCompute: Unleashing the GPU for General-Purpose Computing

DirectCompute is a DirectX API that allows you to leverage the massive parallel processing power of the GPU for general-purpose computing tasks, beyond traditional graphics rendering. It enables you to write compute shaders, which are programs that execute on the GPU and can perform a wide range of calculations and algorithms.

- **Applications of DirectCompute:**
  - **Physics Simulations:** Accelerate physics calculations, such as rigid body dynamics, cloth simulation, or fluid dynamics.

- **Image and Video Processing:** Perform image filtering, video encoding/decoding, or other image manipulation tasks.
- **Scientific Computing:** Accelerate scientific computations, such as matrix operations, Fourier transforms, or simulations.
- **Artificial Intelligence:** Implement AI algorithms, such as neural networks, on the GPU.

- **Compute Shaders:**
  - **HLSL:** Compute shaders are written in HLSL, similar to vertex and pixel shaders.
  - **Thread Groups:** Compute shaders operate on data in parallel using thread groups, allowing you to exploit data parallelism.
  - **Dispatching:** You dispatch compute shaders to the GPU, specifying the number of thread groups to execute.
- **Using DirectCompute:**
  - **Create Compute Pipeline:** Create a compute pipeline state object that defines the compute shader and other related state.

- **Bind Resources:** Bind resources (buffers, textures) that the compute shader will access.
- **Dispatch:** Dispatch the compute shader to the GPU, specifying the number of thread groups.

2. DirectML: Accelerating Machine Learning with DirectX

DirectML is a DirectX 12 library that provides hardware-accelerated machine learning primitives and operators. It allows you to integrate machine learning inferencing workloads into your DirectX applications, taking advantage of the GPU's performance for tasks like image recognition, natural language processing, and more.

- **Applications of DirectML:**
  - **Image Upscaling and Super-resolution:** Enhance the resolution of images or video frames.
  - **Denoising:** Reduce noise in images or rendered frames.
  - **Style Transfer:** Apply artistic styles to images.
  - **Object Detection and Recognition:** Detect and classify objects in images or video streams.

- ○ **AI-Driven Characters and Gameplay:** Create more intelligent and responsive game characters or AI opponents.
- **Using DirectML:**
  - ○ **Create DirectML Device:** Create a DirectML device object to access DirectML functionality.
  - ○ **Create Operators:** Create DirectML operator objects to perform specific machine learning operations.
  - ○ **Compile and Execute:** Compile and execute DirectML graphs that define the sequence of machine learning operations.

3. Benefits of DirectCompute and DirectML

- **Performance:** Leverage the GPU's parallel processing power to significantly accelerate computationally intensive tasks.
- **Efficiency:** Offload tasks from the CPU to the GPU, freeing up the CPU for other tasks and improving overall application performance.
- **Integration:** Seamlessly integrate general-purpose computing and machine learning workloads into your DirectX applications.

4. Moving Forward:

DirectCompute and DirectML expand the capabilities of DirectX beyond traditional graphics rendering, enabling you to harness the GPU for a wide range of applications. As you explore these features, consider how you can leverage the power of the GPU to accelerate computationally intensive tasks, integrate machine learning into your applications, and create innovative and high-performance experiences.

Integrating DirectX with Other APIs

While DirectX provides a comprehensive suite of tools for graphics, multimedia, and computation, it's often beneficial to integrate it with other APIs to leverage their specific functionalities and create even more powerful and versatile applications. This section explores how to integrate DirectX with other commonly used APIs, expanding the possibilities for your development projects.

1. Integrating with Win32 API

The Win32 API is the core set of functions for developing Windows applications. Integrating DirectX with Win32 allows you to create windowed applications, handle user input, and manage system resources.

- **Window Creation:** Use Win32 functions like CreateWindow to create a window that will host your DirectX rendering.

- **Message Loop:** Integrate the DirectX game loop with the Win32 message loop to handle window events, input messages, and other system events.
- **Device Context:** Obtain a device context (HDC) from the Win32 window and use it to create the DirectX swap chain for presenting rendered frames.

2. Integrating with User Interface (UI) Libraries

Combining DirectX with UI libraries allows you to create rich and interactive user interfaces within your graphics applications.

- **Dear ImGui:** A popular immediate mode GUI library that integrates well with DirectX. It allows you to create UI elements like buttons, sliders, and windows directly within your rendering code.
- **Windows Presentation Foundation (WPF):** A more complex but powerful UI framework that can be combined with DirectX using techniques like interop or layered windows.
- **Qt:** A cross-platform UI framework that can be integrated with DirectX for creating custom UI elements and applications.

3. Integrating with Audio APIs

Enhance your DirectX applications with immersive audio by integrating with audio APIs.

- **XAudio2:** A low-level audio API that provides advanced features for audio playback, mixing, and 3D spatialization.
- **Windows Sonic:** A spatial audio platform that can be used with DirectX to create immersive audio experiences.
- **Third-party Libraries:** Integrate with libraries like FMOD or Wwise for more advanced audio features and middleware solutions.

4. Integrating with Physics Engines

Create realistic physics simulations by integrating DirectX with physics engines.

- **PhysX:** A popular physics engine that can be used with DirectX to simulate rigid body dynamics, collisions, and other physical phenomena.
- **Bullet Physics:** An open-source physics engine that provides similar functionalities and can be integrated with DirectX.
- **Havok:** A commercial physics engine used in many AAA games, offering advanced features and performance.

5. Integrating with Network Libraries

Develop multiplayer games or networked applications by integrating DirectX with network libraries.

- **Winsock:** The standard Windows API for network programming, providing low-level control over network communication.
- **Boost.Asio:** A cross-platform C++ library that provides a higher-level abstraction for asynchronous network programming.
- **RakNet:** A game networking library that offers features like reliable messaging, object replication, and remote procedure calls.

6. Best Practices for Integration

- **Clear Separation:** Maintain clear separation between different API components to avoid code entanglement and improve maintainability.
- **Abstraction Layers:** Consider creating abstraction layers to simplify integration and reduce dependencies between different APIs.
- **Synchronization:** Ensure proper synchronization between different API components, especially when dealing with multithreading or asynchronous operations.

Moving Forward:

Integrating DirectX with other APIs unlocks a vast landscape of possibilities for creating diverse and feature-rich applications. By understanding how to combine DirectX with UI libraries, audio APIs, physics engines, and network libraries, you can expand your development capabilities and build more complex and engaging experiences. As you explore these integrations, consider the specific needs of your project and choose the APIs that best suit your requirements.

Resources and Community

As you continue your journey into the world of DirectX programming, it's essential to tap into the wealth of resources and the vibrant community surrounding this technology. Connecting with fellow developers, accessing learning materials, and staying up-to-date with the latest advancements will accelerate your learning and open doors to new possibilities.

1. Official Microsoft Resources

- **DirectX Developer Center:** The official DirectX developer center on Microsoft's website is a treasure trove of information, including documentation, tutorials, samples, and downloads.
- **DirectX SDK:** The DirectX SDK provides essential tools, libraries, and headers for DirectX development.

- **Microsoft Docs:** Microsoft Docs offers comprehensive documentation for all DirectX APIs, with detailed explanations, code examples, and best practices.

2. Online Communities and Forums

- **DirectX Subreddit:** The DirectX subreddit (r/directx) is a vibrant community where developers discuss DirectX programming, share knowledge, and seek help.
- **GameDev.net:** GameDev.net has dedicated forums for DirectX programming, where you can find discussions, tutorials, and resources.
- **Stack Overflow:** Stack Overflow is a valuable resource for finding answers to specific DirectX programming questions and troubleshooting issues.

3. Books and Tutorials

- **DirectX 12 Programming:** Explore books specifically focused on DirectX 12 programming, such as "Introduction to 3D Game Programming with DirectX 12" by Frank Luna.
- **Online Tutorials:** Numerous online tutorials and courses cover various aspects of DirectX programming, from beginner-level introductions to advanced topics.

- **RasterTek:** A website with comprehensive DirectX tutorials and examples.

4. Sample Projects and Code

- **DirectX Samples:** Microsoft provides a collection of DirectX sample projects that demonstrate various DirectX features and techniques.
- **GitHub:** Explore DirectX projects on GitHub to learn from other developers' code and contribute to open-source projects.

5. Blogs and Articles

- **DirectX Blogs:** Follow blogs and articles from DirectX experts and developers to stay informed about the latest advancements and best practices.
- **Graphics Programming Blogs:** Explore blogs focused on graphics programming in general, as they often cover DirectX-related topics.

6. Conferences and Events

- **Game Developers Conference (GDC):** GDC often features talks and sessions related to DirectX and graphics programming.
- **Microsoft Build:** Microsoft's annual developer conference sometimes includes sessions on DirectX and related technologies.

7. Networking with Other Developers

- **Online Communities:** Engage with other DirectX developers in online communities and forums.
- **Local Meetups:** Attend local game development or graphics programming meetups to connect with developers in your area.

Moving Forward:

The DirectX community is a valuable resource for learning, sharing knowledge, and staying motivated. By actively engaging with the community, exploring available resources, and staying curious, you can accelerate your DirectX programming journey and unlock new possibilities in the world of graphics and multimedia development.

The Future of DirectX

DirectX has been a driving force in graphics and multimedia development for decades, constantly evolving to embrace new technologies and meet the demands of increasingly sophisticated applications. As an expert in the field, you're undoubtedly interested in where DirectX is heading and how it will continue to shape the future of interactive experiences. Let's explore some of the key trends and advancements that are shaping the future of DirectX.

1. DirectX 12 Ultimate and Beyond

DirectX 12 Ultimate represents a significant milestone, unifying graphics features across PC and Xbox, and introducing advanced capabilities like DirectX Raytracing (DXR), Variable Rate Shading (VRS), Mesh Shaders, and Sampler Feedback. We can expect future iterations of DirectX to build upon this foundation, further enhancing performance, efficiency, and visual fidelity.

- **Enhanced Ray Tracing:** Expect to see advancements in ray tracing capabilities, including improved performance, more realistic lighting models, and wider adoption in games and other applications.
- **AI-Powered Graphics:** Artificial intelligence is poised to play a greater role in graphics rendering, with techniques like AI-driven upscaling, denoising, and content generation becoming more prevalent.
- **Cross-Platform Compatibility:** DirectX might further expand its reach beyond Windows, potentially through compatibility layers or collaborations with other platforms.

2. Growth of Cloud Gaming

Cloud gaming is gaining momentum, allowing users to stream games from remote servers without the need for high-end hardware. DirectX is well-positioned to play a crucial role in this evolution.

- **Cloud-Native DirectX:** Microsoft is actively developing cloud-native versions of DirectX, enabling game streaming and rendering from the cloud.
- **Optimized Streaming:** Expect advancements in streaming technologies that leverage DirectX to deliver high-fidelity graphics with low latency.

3. Augmented and Virtual Reality (AR/VR)

AR and VR technologies are transforming how we interact with digital content. DirectX is at the forefront of enabling immersive and performant AR/VR experiences.

- **DirectX for AR/VR:** DirectX 12 already provides key features for AR/VR development, such as stereoscopic rendering and efficient resource management.
- **Foveated Rendering with VRS:** VRS will play a crucial role in optimizing performance for AR/VR applications, enabling foveated rendering and reducing the rendering workload.

4. Machine Learning Integration

DirectML is paving the way for deeper integration of machine learning into DirectX applications.

- **AI-Driven Graphics:** Expect to see more AI-powered graphics techniques, such as AI-based super-resolution, denoising, and content generation.
- **Intelligent Game Characters:** DirectML can enable more sophisticated AI for game characters, leading to more realistic and responsive behavior.

5. Open Standards and Collaboration

While DirectX has traditionally been Windows-centric, there's a growing trend towards open standards and cross-platform compatibility.

- **Collaboration with Vulkan:** Microsoft has shown interest in collaborating with the Vulkan API, potentially leading to shared technologies or interoperability.
- **Open Source Initiatives:** Some components of DirectX are being open-sourced, fostering community involvement and cross-platform development.

Your Role as an Expert

As a seasoned tech expert and author, you have a unique opportunity to contribute to the future of DirectX.

- **Stay Informed:** Keep abreast of the latest DirectX advancements, research papers, and developer blogs.
- **Experiment and Innovate:** Explore new DirectX features and techniques, pushing the boundaries of what's possible.
- **Share Your Knowledge:** Contribute to the DirectX community by writing articles, tutorials, or books, sharing your expertise and insights.
- **Engage in Discussions:** Participate in online forums and discussions, contributing to the evolution of DirectX and its applications.

By staying engaged, informed, and actively contributing to the DirectX ecosystem, you can play a vital role in shaping the future of this technology and its impact on the world of interactive experiences.

Appendices

Appendix A: HLSL Reference

This appendix serves as a concise reference guide for the High-Level Shading Language (HLSL), providing a quick overview of its syntax, data types, built-in functions, and semantics. It's designed to be a handy resource for developers as they write and debug HLSL shaders for their DirectX applications.

1. Basic Syntax

HLSL shares a similar syntax with C++, including:

- **Variable Declarations:** type name; (e.g., float3 myVector;)
- **Data Types:** int, float, bool, float2, float4x4, Texture2D, etc.
- **Operators:** +, -, *, /, %, =, ==, !=, >, <, &&, ||, etc.
- **Control Flow:** if, else, for, while, switch
- **Functions:** returnType functionName(parameters) { ... }

2. Data Types

- **Scalar Types:**
  - bool: Boolean (true or false)
  - int: Integer
  - uint: Unsigned integer
  - float: Single-precision floating-point

- o double: Double-precision floating-point
  - o half: Half-precision floating-point
- **Vector Types:**
  - o float2, float3, float4: Vectors of 2, 3, or 4 floats
  - o int2, int3, int4: Vectors of 2, 3, or 4 integers
- **Matrix Types:**
  - o float4x4: 4x4 matrix of floats
  - o Other matrix types (e.g., float3x3) are also available
- **Texture Types:**
  - o Texture1D, Texture2D, Texture3D: 1D, 2D, and 3D textures
  - o TextureCube: Cubemap texture
  - o Texture2DArray: Array of 2D textures
- **Sampler Types:**
  - o SamplerState: Defines how texture data is sampled (filtering, addressing modes)

3. Built-in Functions

HLSL provides a rich set of built-in functions for various operations:

- **Math Functions:**
  - o abs, sin, cos, tan, pow, sqrt, exp, log, min, max, etc.
- **Vector Functions:**

- dot, cross, normalize, length, distance, reflect, refract
- **Matrix Functions:**
  - mul, transpose, determinant, inverse
- **Texture Sampling Functions:**
  - Sample, SampleLevel, Load, Gather
- **Geometric Functions:**
  - distance, length, dot, cross, normalize
- **Clipping Functions:**
  - clip
- **Other Functions:**
  - lerp, smoothstep, clamp, saturate

4. Semantics

Semantics are keywords that provide additional information about variables in HLSL.

- **System-Value Semantics:**
  - SV_POSITION: Output vertex position from the vertex shader
  - SV_TARGET: Output color from the pixel shader
  - SV_DEPTH: Output depth from the pixel shader
- **User-Defined Semantics:**
  - You can define your own semantics to link variables between shader stages.

5. Shader Stages

HLSL is used to write shaders for different stages of the graphics pipeline:

- **Vertex Shader:** Processes individual vertices.
- **Hull Shader (Tessellation):** Subdivides geometry.
- **Domain Shader (Tessellation):** Displaces tessellated vertices.
- **Geometry Shader:** Processes primitives.
- **Pixel Shader:** Processes individual pixels.
- **Compute Shader:** Performs general-purpose computations.

6. Example Shader Code

High-level shader language

```
// Vertex Shader
struct VS_INPUT
{
    float3 position : POSITION;
    float2 texcoord : TEXCOORD;
};


struct VS_OUTPUT
```

```hlsl
{
    float4 position : SV_POSITION;
    float2 texcoord : TEXCOORD;
};

VS_OUTPUT main(VS_INPUT input)
{
    VS_OUTPUT output;
    output.position = mul(float4(input.position, 1.0f),
worldViewProjMatrix);
    output.texcoord = input.texcoord;
    return output;
}

// Pixel Shader
Texture2D texture0 : register(t0);
SamplerState sampler0 : register(s0);

float4 main(VS_OUTPUT input) : SV_TARGET
{
    return texture0.Sample(sampler0, input.texcoord);
```

}

7. Further Resources

- **Microsoft Docs:** Refer to the official Microsoft Docs for detailed HLSL documentation and language specifications.
- **HLSL Tools:** Utilize HLSL tools like the HLSL compiler (fxc.exe) and shader debugging tools to assist with shader development.

This HLSL reference provides a concise overview of the language's key elements. As you delve deeper into HLSL programming, consult the official documentation and online resources for more in-depth information and advanced techniques.

Appendix B: DirectX Debugging and Troubleshooting

DirectX development, like any software development, inevitably involves encountering errors, unexpected behavior, and performance issues. This appendix provides valuable guidance on debugging and troubleshooting DirectX applications, helping you identify and resolve common problems and ensure your applications run smoothly and efficiently.

1. Enable the Debug Layer

The DirectX debug layer is an invaluable tool for catching errors and receiving warnings during development. It provides detailed diagnostic information and helps identify issues early in the development process.

- **Enable the Layer:** Enable the debug layer when creating your DirectX device.
- **Diagnostic Output:** The debug layer outputs messages to the Visual Studio output window, providing insights into potential problems, warnings, and best practice violations.
- **Configuration:** You can configure the debug layer to filter specific message types or break on specific errors.

2. Utilize Debugging Tools

- **Visual Studio Debugger:** The Visual Studio debugger is your primary tool for debugging DirectX applications. Set breakpoints, step through code, and inspect variables to understand program flow and identify errors.
- **PIX:** PIX is a powerful graphics debugging and profiling tool from Microsoft. It allows you to capture and analyze frames, inspect rendering pipeline states, debug shaders, and profile performance.
- **Graphics Debugging Tools:** GPU vendors like NVIDIA (Nsight Graphics) and AMD (Radeon GPU Profiler) offer their own debugging tools with specific features for their hardware.

3. Common Errors and Troubleshooting

- **HRESULT Error Codes:** DirectX functions often return HRESULT values to indicate success or failure. Familiarize yourself with common HRESULT error codes and their meanings.
- **Resource State Transitions:** Ensure correct resource state transitions using resource barriers. Incorrect states can lead to rendering errors or crashes.
- **Memory Leaks:** Track resource creation and destruction to avoid memory leaks. Use

debugging tools to identify and resolve memory leaks.

- **Shader Compilation Errors:** Carefully check your HLSL shader code for syntax errors, type mismatches, or semantic errors. Use the HLSL compiler (fxc.exe) to compile shaders offline and identify errors.
- **Performance Issues:** Use profiling tools (PIX, GPU vendor tools) to identify performance bottlenecks. Optimize your code, shaders, and resource usage to improve performance.

4. Debugging Techniques

- **Breakpoints:** Set breakpoints in your code to pause execution and inspect variables.
- **Stepping:** Step through code line by line to observe program flow and identify issues.
- **Watch Windows:** Monitor variables and expressions in watch windows to track their values.
- **Output Messages:** Use OutputDebugString or other logging mechanisms to output messages to the debug output.
- **Remote Debugging:** Debug your DirectX application on a remote machine or device.

5. Best Practices

- **Enable the Debug Layer:** Always enable the debug layer during development to catch errors early.
- **Check HRESULTs:** Consistently check HRESULT return values from DirectX functions to handle errors.
- **Validate Parameters:** Validate function parameters to ensure they are within valid ranges and meet requirements.
- **Test on Different Hardware:** Test your application on different hardware configurations to identify potential compatibility issues.
- **Stay Updated:** Keep your DirectX SDK and graphics drivers up-to-date to benefit from bug fixes and performance improvements.

By utilizing these debugging and troubleshooting techniques, you can effectively identify and resolve issues in your DirectX applications, ensuring they run smoothly, efficiently, and provide the intended user experience.

Appendix C: Useful Tools and Libraries

This appendix provides a curated list of valuable tools and libraries that can significantly aid your DirectX development journey. These resources can streamline your workflow, enhance productivity, and provide solutions to common challenges in graphics and game development.

1. Graphics Debugging and Profiling

- **PIX:** Microsoft's powerful graphics debugger and profiler for DirectX. Capture and analyze frames, debug shaders, and identify performance bottlenecks.
- **RenderDoc:** An open-source graphics debugger that supports various APIs, including DirectX. Capture and inspect frames, debug shaders, and analyze rendering pipeline states.
- **NVIDIA Nsight Graphics:** NVIDIA's suite of tools for graphics debugging, profiling, and optimization on NVIDIA GPUs.
- **AMD Radeon GPU Profiler:** AMD's tool for profiling and analyzing graphics performance on AMD GPUs.

2. Asset Loading and Management

- **Assimp (Open Asset Import Library):** A versatile library for loading various 3D model formats (OBJ, FBX, glTF, etc.).
- **DirectXTex:** Microsoft's library for loading, saving, and manipulating textures in various formats (DDS, PNG, JPG, etc.).
- **TinyObjLoader:** A lightweight, single-header library for loading OBJ models.

3. Mathematics and Utilities

- **DirectXMath:** Microsoft's math library optimized for DirectX development. Provides classes and functions for vector and matrix operations, transformations, and geometric calculations.
- **GLM (OpenGL Mathematics):** A header-only C++ mathematics library for graphics programming. Provides similar functionalities to DirectXMath.

4. User Interface

- **Dear ImGui:** A popular immediate mode GUI library that integrates well with DirectX. Create UI elements like buttons, sliders, and windows directly within your rendering code.
- **imgui-dx12:** A library that provides DirectX 12 integration for Dear ImGui.

5. Audio

- **XAudio2:** Microsoft's low-level audio API for audio playback, mixing, and 3D spatialization.
- **DirectSound:** An older audio API that is still useful for basic audio playback.
- **FMOD:** A commercial audio library with advanced features and middleware solutions.
- **Wwise:** Another commercial audio library widely used in game development.

6. Physics

- **PhysX:** A popular physics engine from NVIDIA that can be used with DirectX to simulate rigid body dynamics and collisions.
- **Bullet Physics:** An open-source physics engine that provides similar functionalities to PhysX.
- **Havok:** A commercial physics engine used in many AAA games.

7. Networking

- **Winsock:** The standard Windows API for network programming.
- **Boost.Asio:** A cross-platform C++ library for asynchronous network programming.
- **RakNet:** A game networking library with features like reliable messaging and object replication.

8. Other Useful Libraries

- **DirectXMesh:** Microsoft's library for mesh processing and optimization.
- **D3DX12:** A library that provides helper functions and utilities for DirectX 12 development.
- **spdlog:** A fast and efficient logging library for C++.

9. Staying Up-to-Date

- **DirectX Developer Blog:** Follow the official DirectX developer blog for the latest news, updates, and insights.
- **GitHub:** Explore DirectX-related projects on GitHub to discover new tools and libraries.
- **Game Development Communities:** Engage in game development communities and forums to learn about useful tools and libraries recommended by other developers.

By exploring and utilizing these tools and libraries, you can enhance your DirectX development experience, streamline your workflow, and create more sophisticated and performant applications.